THE COUNTRYSIDE IN QUESTION

THE COUNTRYSIDE IN QUESTION

HOWARD NEWBY

HUTCHINSON

London Melbourne Auckland Johannesburg

Hutchinson

An imprint of Century Hutchinson Ltd

62–65 Chandos Place, London WC2N 4NW

Century Hutchinson Australia Pty Ltd
PO Box 496, 16–22 Church Street, Hawthorn,
Victoria 3122, Australia

Century Hutchinson New Zealand Ltd
PO Box 40–086, Glenfield, Auckland 10,
New Zealand

Century Hutchinson South Africa (Pty) Ltd
PO Box 337, Berglvei 2012, South Africa

First published 1988

© Howard Newby 1988

Set in Bembo Roman
by Deltatype Ltd, Ellesmere Port

Designed by Nancy Lawrence

Illustrated by Chris Evans

Printed in Great Britain by
Butler & Tanner Ltd, Frome and London

British Library Cataloguing in Publication Data
Newby, Howard, *1947 –*
   The countryside in question.
   1.Country life — Great Britain
   I. Title
   941.009′734   S522.G7

   ISBN 0 09 173104 6 cased
         0 09 172950 5 paper

ACKNOWLEDGEMENTS

The Author and publishers are grateful to the copyright holders listed below for their kind permission to reproduce the following material:

Countryside Commission for pages 112, 120, 122, 125, also 126 by Colin Horsman, 127 by Charles Meechan, 129, 132 by Mike Williams, and 131 by David Winpenny.

Simon Crouch for the frontispiece and pages viii, 11, 14, 15, 19, 53, 58, 61 and colour plate 3.

Tessa Harris for pages 4, 29, 71, 74, 116, 119.

HTV West for pages vi by Charles Boulton, and pages 24, 50, 78, 85, 90 by Brian Morgan, also the contents page and pages 30, 37, 38, 45, 47, 49, 57, 65, 66, 86, 92, 95, 97, 99, 100, 105, 108, 110, 111, 134, 146, 148 and colour plates 1 2, and 4 by Stuart Sadd.

Hywel James for pages 7, 8, 21, 27.

N. R. Lawrence for pages 12, 32, 55, 64, 150, 152.

Rosy Massil for pages 41, 63, 82, 137.

Peak Park Joint Planning Board for pages 141 and 143.

Susan Wilson for page 69.

The Author and publishers would like to particularly thank Millie Hunt for the use of her material on pages 43, 44, 46, 48, 50.

CONTENTS

PREFACE

THIS BOOK IS DESIGNED TO accompany the television series *The Countryside in Question*, produced and directed by Adrian Brenard for HTV. I was responsible for scripting and presenting the series and it should be emphasized that the opinions presented in that series and in this book are mine alone.

Readers who wish to explore further the issues raised here can do so in two of my previous books, *Green and Pleasant Land?* (second edition published by Wildwood House, 1986), and *Country Life* (Weidenfeld, 1987). Further reading is listed at the end of this book.

It is a happy duty to thank many of those to whom I owe a debt of gratitude for what follows. At HTV David Alexander had the original idea for the series and took the risk of inviting me to become involved. Adrian Brenard turned my distinctly non-televisual scripts into something watchable: my debt to him is enormous. I also learned a considerable amount from the rest of the HTV crew during many soggy weeks on location during what passed for the summer of 1987, especially Sarah Varaillon, Brian Morgan, Gordon Kethro, Micky Spiller, and Hywel James. My thanks to them and all the others involved in leavening their professionalism with patience and good humour. Thanks also to Frances Kelly, my literary agent, and to Claire L'Enfant, my publisher at Century Hutchinson.

Finally, a few words are necessary in order to define the scope of this book. By no means all of the issues facing the future of the British countryside are included. The book has closely followed the format of the television series and there is only so much material that can be included in six half-hour programmes. Moreover, for production reasons filming was not undertaken in Scotland. Consequently this book, too, pays insufficient attention to specifically Scottish issues and so the term 'British' needs to be understood with that proviso.

INTRODUCTION

THE BRITISH COUNTRYSIDE: serene, timeless, immemorial – a source of peaceful certainty in an ever-changing and uncertain modern world. Rural Britain holds a special place in our affections. It seems to contain all that is best in Britain and Britishness. From it we draw a sense of our history, our culture, our very identity as a nation. The countryside reassures us that not everything these days is superficial and transitory, but that some things remain stable, permanent and enduring. In rural Britain, we like to believe, it is still possible to maintain a proper perspective on life, to rediscover our sense of harmony with nature and our sense of peace with our fellow human beings.

Today the temptation to escape from the turmoil of our cities into the peace and quiet of the countryside has seldom appeared more attractive and more desirable. Somewhere, we hope, beyond the tower blocks and the traffic jams, where the motorways and the electricity pylons have not yet reached, it is possible to escape from the urban rat-race and find happy country folk living in the midst of 'real' countryside. It is an image which is becoming ever more popular. For rural Britain has become a kind of retreat for most of us, a place where we can retain our sanity by 'getting away from it all' amidst a remote rural fastness. It is a place where we can recharge our emotional batteries and rediscover our roots.

We jealously preserve this image of the countryside as the reality of our daily lives becomes more difficult and depressing. Any threat to our rural heritage – its beauty, its landscape, its ancient villages, its wildlife – meets with an understandable outcry. It is little wonder that preservation and conservation have emerged as the watchwords of public debate in recent years. Once the countryside is viewed as the repository of all

that we cherish and hold dear, then it is not surprising that many of us wish fiercely to guard and protect it.

But how far is our idyllic image of the countryside matched by the present reality? Sometimes the image appears fragile so that our love of the countryside is often accompanied by a deep foreboding. Behind the picturesque view does there lurk something less pleasant? The countryside may be the repository of our 'heritage', but it is also the countryside of tower silos, asbestos barns, up-rooted hedgerows, ploughed-up moorland, burning stubble, pesticides, factory farming and genetic engineering. Viewed from this perspective the countryside is under threat. Can the countryside as we know it survive as a haven of peace and quiet? What kind of countryside will we have as we move towards the twenty-first century?

In order to answer questions like these we need to take a more dispassionate look at what is actually happening in the countryside. Sometimes our idyllic image stops us seeing the reality. There is certainly a lot to be concerned about. An informed public debate about the future of rural Britain is urgently needed, for the countryside is facing the most widespread set of changes since before the Second World War. The future of the countryside hangs in the balance. Yet unless we can penetrate the haze of sentiment and nostalgia which hangs over prevailing public perceptions of the countryside such a debate will be undermined by a failure to appreciate the very real changes which are now in train.

Let us look at some of the issues which are revolutionizing the life of our rural areas:

- Technological change in farming has turned Britain into a food-exporting nation for the first time since the end of the eighteenth century. But the same changes have produced huge – and costly – food surpluses in Europe. We can now meet most of our food needs by using much less land for farming. Up to 10 million acres of farmland may be redundant by the 1990s. What is to be done with it?
- The same advances in technology have produced heated conflicts over environmental issues such as landscape change, pollution, the destruction of wildlife habitats, and the welfare of farm animals. Can the efficient production of food be reconciled with conservation of the countryside and the humane treatment of animals?
- With fewer people employed on farms our villages have changed from farming communities into commuter dormitories and weekend retreats. In some places resentment has grown between the 'locals' – concerned about jobs, housing and

rural services – and more affluent 'newcomers' who are generally resistant to change. Can the village survive fewer jobs on the land, planning restrictions on new jobs and housing, and cutbacks in local services?

- Increased leisure time has brought new pressures on the countryside. Most people who live in towns see it as a playspace; farmers view it as as their factory yard; newcomer residents regard it as an escape from the rat-race. So conflict has arisen over access to the countryside, whether on the fringes of urban areas or in the more remote parts of mountains and moors. Should the public have more opportunities to use the countryside for recreation and leisure?

Many of these problems have crept up on us unawares. The public has shown itself eager to learn about the countryside, as the success of *The Archers* and *Emmerdale Farm*, of natural history programmes, and the insatiable demand for books and guides on rural life bear witness. But in many respects a considerable ignorance remains about what the countryside actually contains. Dominant images tend to be either outdated or highly partial. Books on the countryside still feature horse-drawn ploughs, poppy-filled fields, and the district nurse's Morris Minor outside the thatched cottage. Public knowledge of natural history has increased remarkably; but its understanding of agricultural developments remains sketchy. There is a heightened awareness of landscape change and the threats to the ecology of the countryside; but there is less debate about the problems facing the social and economic life of rural communities. Ironically, public understanding of what is happening in the countryside is sometimes alarmingly uninformed, even when the desire to learn is clearly there. Image and reality continue to be at variance.

This book will attempt to close this gap. If rural Britain is indeed at a turning-point in its history, then an informed public debate which can guide the future direction of change is urgently required. We all care deeply about our countryside, but few of us actually live in it. Few of us are – or can be – fully aware of what is going on in the countryside – we all have other, equally valid, preoccupations. Yet the countryside is now undergoing such massive change that within as little as a decade it could – if we are prepared to allow it – become almost unrecognizable from that which is so familiar to us today. If we do care about the future of the countryside we must begin to work out how the various claims which will be made upon it can be reconciled. We should ask ourselves, what kind of countryside do we want?

A GREEN AND PLEASANT LAND?

Wʜᴀᴛ ᴡᴇ sᴇᴇ ᴀs ᴡᴇ ᴘᴀss through the countryside by car or train is overwhelmingly a farmed landscape. The conclusion we draw from this is that rural Britain continues to be dominated by agriculture. But only two out of every hundred people in Britain are engaged in farming – even in rural areas the proportion is rarely more than one in ten. Even if we include the ancillary and food processing industries it is rare for more than one-third of the rural population to be associated with agriculture. This leaves a large majority of the rural population who do not earn their living from, or base their way of life on, farming. Today, farming is important in the countryside because it controls the use of *land*, but future changes in the farming industry will have very little effect on any other aspect of rural life.

If this seems confusing, so in some ways it is. For centuries the economic basis of the British countryside has been farming. The countryside we see around us today is very much a product of the agricultural industry. Appearances can be deceptive, however. Agriculture may be the greatest user of the land in the countryside, but the days when rural Britain could, in any other sense, be considered mainly agricultural have long gone. It is *only* in terms of land use that rural Britain is now agricultural Britain. In all other – and less visible senses – agriculture is no longer dominant. Economically, occupationally, socially, culturally, the countryside has already been comprehensively 'urbanized'. As a result we need a new way of looking (literally as well as figuratively) at rural Britain if we are to perceive the changes already under way.

We must not underestimate the local importance of the farming economy in a few of the remoter parts of Britain. Nor should we play down the impact of farming change on the ecology and landscape of the countryside while agriculture remains a

major land use. But we must look at the role of farming in proper perspective and not be misled by casual observations. It is easy to overlook the most fundamental change which has occurred in recent decades: rural Britain is no longer agricultural Britain.

How has this state of affairs come about? The rural society we possess today is the result of a profound series of changes in farming; but paradoxically the countryside of tomorrow will be affected much less by farming change as a result. Farming will continue to determine how the countryside *looks* but not what it *is*. We need to understand how we got here before we can decide which way to go in the future.

FROM AGRICULTURE TO AGRIBUSINESS

When the older generation of farmers today look back to their childhood and early adulthood, the contrast could hardly be greater. Farming has become less of a dignified and arcadian vocation and more of a business. The traditional rhythms of the farming year remain – but only just. Seed-time is more often in October than in May. Harvest is a matter of days rather than weeks. Farms have become bigger, more mechanized and more specialized. British agriculture, which down to the Second World War was technologically backward and economically depressed, is now not only one of the most efficient, but also one of the most profitable in the world. In four decades British farming has moved decisively from agriculture to agribusiness.

By applying scientific and technological principles to the pursuit of profit and the production of food farming has been revolutionized. The most visible consequence of this has been the change from a mainly horse-and-hand technology to more mechanized systems of production involving the tractor and combine harvester. Other, less visible, innovations have had equally startling effects. Productivity has been boosted by artificial fertilizers and the widespread application of pesticides and other chemicals. Plant and animal breeding have been helped by advances in genetics. More recently farming has moved into the world of biotechnology – genetic engineering, cloning, enzyme technology, and so on. Farmers have been fortunate, for science has served them well. Even now there are plenty of scientific innovations in the pipeline to ensure a further round of increasing productivity in the foreseeable future.

Science has given farmers the tools for the job, but the midwife of this second agricultural revolution has been the state. Successive post-war governments have guaranteed to farmers the conditions that would favour continuing prosperity, and so farmers have known that their efforts to increase productivity would be appropriately

AGRIBUSINESS HAS REVOLUTIONIZED FARMING METHODS
SINCE THE WAR: SLURRY-SPREADING IN PEMBROKESHIRE

rewarded. The guiding philosophy has been the 'Dig for Victory' campaign of wartime Britain, after which the public accepted that 'every acre counts' and that there could be no return to the depression and dereliction of pre-war farming. A grateful nation was taught the value of supporting home-grown food. It is a folk memory that still exerts a great influence over both farmers and the general public today.

The enormous growth of government intervention in agriculture stemmed initially from the necessities of wartime control. Farmers found that they were willing to give up some of their independence in return for stability and prosperity. Public opinion, too, was sympathetic towards farmers, not only in recognition of agriculture's strategic importance, but also in acknowledgement of farming's wartime sacrifices. This consensus was embodied in the Agriculture Act of 1947, the single most influential piece of legislation which governed post-war agricultural policy. From then onwards both the general direction and the detailed implementation of agricultural change was influenced by government policy. For four decades, farmers were supported by the public purse.

After 1947 public support for agriculture was made through an annual price review for particular farming commodities, undertaken by the Ministry of Agriculture in consultation with the farmers' organizations, principally the National Farmers' Union. The price review determined the following year's price guarantees to farmers. If market prices fell below guaranteed prices then farmers received the difference in cash – a 'deficiency payment'. Such payments came out of general taxation, allowing

CEREALS FARMING HAS BEEN MOST AFFECTED BY TECHNOLOGICAL CHANGE.
THE MODERN ARABLE FARMER MUST GET BIG OR GET OUT
LARGE AMOUNTS OF INVESTMENT ARE NOW REQUIRED FOR
MACHINERY WHICH MAY ONLY BE USED ON A FEW DAYS IN A YEAR:
BRINGING IN THE HARVEST IN SUFFOLK

the consumer to take advantage of cheap food prices in the shops. The beauty of this system was that a 'cheap food policy', attractive to urban consumers, was perpetuated, while farmers were able to receive an equitable return. The cost of farm support was not immediately noticeable to the average taxpayer, while the system also contained a hidden welfare element for poor families by supporting cheap food through the payment of taxes.

This policy was so successful that agriculture was taken out of the realm of everyday political controversy until 1973, when Britain entered the European Economic Community. Before 1973 farming policy had been a technical matter, the mysteries of which were familiar only to ministry officials, farmers' representatives and a few academic observers. On the whole the public was content to allow them to get on with it and for thirty years the growth of a stable and efficient agriculture disguised some of the more questionable aspects of the system. By tinkering with the details of guarantees, grants and subsidies, governments could influence farmers through appropriate 'price signals' while allowing them to keep up their role of independent businessmen. This placed the direction of policy further in the hands of technical experts and for a while, at least, the public had little reason to question its fundamental aims.

As a result, agricultural policy came to have one main aim: the production of more and cheaper food. It was spectacularly successful. Forty years later, indeed, it is almost *too* successful: the technological miracle of modern farming has provided us with unprecedented abundance. But each of us can only eat so much food – consumer demand cannot expand indefinitely. Wartime shortages have given way inexorably to chronic surpluses.

Government regulation of agriculture has profoundly altered the nature of day-to-day life and work in the countryside. The encouragement of fewer, larger and more capital-intensive farms has resulted in the catalogue of social and economic changes we see today: the mechanization of agriculture, the exodus of labourers from the farming industry, the changing population of rural villages and the environmental consequences on the landscape and wildlife of the British countryside. These changes have not been haphazard or the result of factors beyond human control. They are the result of deliberate policies. Successive governments have promoted technological change and forced farmers on to a treadmill of expansion, investment and rationalization. This has been a revolution by committee, monitored by the bureaucrat and made possible by the public official. Farmers may act *as if* they were governed by the free market, but the real architect of modern British agriculture has been the state.

Agricultural policy lets farmers know what is required of them by manipulating their costs and prices. For example, in order to goad farmers into increasing their efficiency, the annual price review usually tried to place farmers in a 'cost–price squeeze' – in other words, their increasing costs have not been fully compensated by increases in price. This acts as a spur to farmers to introduce new technology in order to further reduce their costs. But new agricultural technology generally needs larger holdings in order to take full advantage of it, and only the larger farms have been able to generate the resources to invest in it. As a result the larger holdings have been able to obtain cost advantages not available to the small farmer, while the latter has found it increasingly difficult to survive. The size of farm which can generate sufficient income to support a full-time farmer has nearly doubled each decade since the war.

The result is that farmers have had to 'get big or get out'. Because support has been paid on the basis of output, the bulk of public assistance has found its way to the large-scale producer. Efficiency has been on a collision course with equity: those who have received the bulk of the support are arguably those who have needed it least. The outcome has been the increasing concentration of production on fewer, larger farms. Moreover, traditional mixed farming has declined as farmers have sought to spread the cost of specialized new technologies over a greater volume of production. One by-product is that traditional crop and livestock rotations have been displaced by intensive monoculture – growing the same crop year after year.

Although farms have in general been increasing in size, the pace of change has been far from uniform. In some branches of production, such as dairy farming and sheep production, most economies of scale are within the reach of the family farm. As the average size of farms has increased, at the same time a 'dual farming structure' has slowly emerged. On the one hand, a highly capitalized and large-scale 'agribusiness' sector has gained increasing control over cereals and intensive livestock production. Here factory farming, which before the war would have been regarded as a contradiction in terms, has become relatively commonplace. Numerically this sector is quite small – not much more than 10 per cent of all farmers – but commercially it is in the ascendancy, accounting for nearly two-thirds of the output from British farms. The second sector is numerically much larger, but commercially less significant, consisting of small and part-time farmers, making a living where they can.

In practice there is little *direct* competition between the two. The small farming sector continues to hang on, often by dint of economic flexibility and personal tenacity – although, of course, today's small farmer is often yesterday's large one. The

whole thrust of post-war policy has put the long-term survival of the small farm in jeopardy: their disappearance is the price to be paid for increasing efficiency. Yet the small farming sector is the one which has held most appeal for the population at large. Post-war policy has had the aim of driving the small farmer out of business, but this has rarely been spelt out. The drive towards rational farming has been tempered by an acknowledgement of the crucial role played by the small farming sector in supporting the fabric of rural communities.

The clearest case of social, as opposed to economic support, has been the special payments made to hill farmers since 1946. The Hill Farming Act of that year recognized the threat to upland communities unless 'uneconomic' hill farmers were given special help to keep them in business. The act allowed 'headage' payments to be made to sheep and cattle farmers in designated hill areas – in effect a direct subsidy on the cost of production. The motive was social welfare rather than the promotion of efficiency. Nevertheless, hill farmers were not shielded from the general tendencies of post-war policy. Neither social need nor environmental hardship were used as the basis of payments, but gross output. Here, too, the more farmers produced, the greater their total subsidy – so the uplands have experienced the same concentration of production on fewer, larger farms.

Small farmers, whether in the uplands or the lowlands, have been an embarrassment for post-war policy-makers. They have proved to be a stubborn obstacle to the sweep towards a rationalized farming structure. Their regional concentration in the north and west of Britain has, however, made them impossible to ignore. As we look towards the future, the role of the small farmer is likely to come under scrutiny once more. Will they be able to muster the support they need? Or if cost of farming support is to be reduced, will the small farmer once more become expendable?

TRADITIONAL UPLAND FARMING: SHEEP-SHEARING IN THE LAKE DISTRICT

RECENT ATTEMPTS TO RESTRICT EXPENDITURE ON FARM
SUPPORT HAVE HIT CATTLE PRODUCTION THE MOST.
SURVEYING A TROUBLED FUTURE IN NIDDERDALE, YORKSHIRE

This question lies at the heart of the difficulty which British agricultural policy has found in adapting to the Common Agricultural Policy (CAP) of the EEC since 1973. The CAP was specifically designed both to keep the small farmer in production and as a tool for the general development of rural areas. Both objectives were (and are) opposed to established British policy practice. Moreover, the basis of support has switched from general taxation (via deficiency payments) to consumer prices (via direct market intervention). This was guaranteed to drag the debate on farm support away from the backwaters of technical discussion into the full glare of the political and public arena. For the farmer, entry into the EEC proved, in the short term, to be almost embarrassingly beneficial in most areas of production. Price levels which were fixed in order to give a European peasant a reasonable living were bound to be generous indeed to a barley baron in southern England. Every incentive was now offered to expand production.

The longer-term consequences have been less favourable, however. Consumer resentment towards farmers has built up behind the dam of rising food prices. As a matter of policy the CAP 'protects' Europe from cheap food available in the rest of the world. In Britain, the abandonment of a cheap food policy has produced a growing public antagonism towards 'feather-bedded' farmers. To the average shopper in Tesco's or Sainsbury's it makes no sense to support farmers in producing unwanted surpluses of grain, milk, beef, etc., which are then stored at great expense to the taxpayer before being sold below cost price, usually to Eastern Europe. The political consequences of this are still being worked through. On the one hand, the consumer demands cheap food – and thereby gives an added push in favour of agribusiness and the disappearance of the small farmer. On the other hand, the small farmer attracts sympathy as a deserving case for public support while agribusinessmen are resented. Farmers, not surprisingly, feel that the public cannot have it both ways.

Forty years after the existing system of farm support was enshrined in legislation, agricultural policy is at a crossroads. There has been some determination in Whitehall, if not in Brussels, to dismantle many of the public supports for farmers and to allow the cold chill of market forces to blow once more across the industry. Farmers feel beleaguered and misunderstood. As they see it, their only sin has been to achieve the aims which the public has set out for them. Now that they have expanded their production and increased their efficiency, they feel betrayed by a public which is turning its back on them. But the political realities of the 1980s have ordained that the government is no longer prepared to support the production of a commodity for

SMALL FARMERS IN THE HILLS HAVE BENEFITED LEAST
FROM THE SYSTEM OF POST-WAR SUPPORT. WHEN FARMERS
GIVE UP THE STRUGGLE DEPOPULATION AND
DERELICTION RESULT. NENTHEAD, CUMBRIA

which there is no discernible market. Even social justifications can be swept aside: ask the steelworkers, the shipbuilders or the coalminers. 'Green miners' has been an epithet used against the farming community.

Agriculture is ripe for restructuring, yet the debate about what kind of farming structure we want has barely begun. This question was also asked in the 1940s and answered with resounding unanimity. But the conditions of the 1980s are very different. We no longer need to 'Dig for Victory'; we no longer need every acre; the next war will not be fought via submarine warfare in the western approaches. Four decades on, the traditional basis of Britain's farming policy has ebbed away. Britain needs an efficient farming industry, but it does not need so much of it. As a nation we have to ask ourselves what kind of farming structure we want, and how much we are prepared to pay for it.

HOW LONG CAN MARGINAL FARMING SURVIVE?

——— A TALE OF THREE FARMERS ———

Farming does not consist of abstract trends and airy generalizations. Farming is also a patchwork of family histories, hopes and aspirations. The relentless pursuit of efficient farming could mean over 10,000 bankruptcies in the industry by the end of the decade. Each one will be a personal tragedy to set beside the impersonal accumulation of farming statistics. So what do these general trends in farming mean, literally, on the ground? Let us look at what these changes mean for three different farming families.

——— JOHN KERR ———

John Kerr farms over 4000 acres of land in East Suffolk, north of Ipswich. The bulk of the land is used for growing cereals, primarily winter wheat and winter barley, but he also grows large amounts of sugar beet, potatoes and field vegetables (mostly peas and dwarf beans on contract for freezing). Because part of his land lies in the valley of the river Deben, John Kerr also keeps a sizeable dairy herd of 250 cows with an EEC production quota of 1.5 million litres. In addition he fattens 30,000 'bootiful' turkeys and runs a successful farm park which attracts over 50,000 visitors each year. He employs twenty-seven full-time workers, but several times that number of casual and seasonal workers, depending upon the time of the year.

John Kerr detests the term 'agribusinessman' and regards himself as a family farmer who has expanded his business in order to maintain employment for his workforce, rather than allow his workers to become redundant. Certainly, like the vast majority of large-scale farmers, the business is run by and for the family. John's father, William Kerr, established the farm in 1938. He was one of a number of Scottish farmers who migrated to East Anglia during the depression years in order to find land which was unavailable at home. By a mixture of thrift, hard work and shrewd business acumen they were able to make a success of farming where the less efficient and somewhat backward-looking natives had failed. William Kerr left Ayrshire shortly after his honeymoon and rented a 400 acre farm at Easton, Suffolk, which as he still recalls, was in a 'shocking state'. In his first year he grew 70 acres of sugar beet – a crop he had never handled before.

For William Kerr, like many other farmers, the war brought opportunities for expansion. The supply of milk for the retail market provided a secure basis from which to expand the business into vegetables and cereals. This pattern continued after the war. In 1954 William Kerr was able to purchase two of the farms which he had hitherto rented – 640 acres in all. Other 'bits and pieces' have been added until now the family owns 1500 acres, while farming the remaining 2500 under a variety of leases, management agreements and consultancies. William Kerr still recalls the 'big step' of purchasing his first combine harvester and replacing his Suffolk horses with Fordson tractors. (The stables now form part of the farm park, to which the Suffolks have returned, and the old tractors are part of a museum.)

William Kerr has now retired, although he remains chairman of the family farming company. His son John is in day-to-day charge of the business, assisted by a young

farm manager. John Kerr recognizes that his outlook on farming has been influenced by his own family experience, and as a result he has been conditioned to think in terms of expansion. Until very recently, governments had exhorted him to expand production. He has increased the size of the dairy herd, increased milk yields, expanded the production of crops with the assistance of new technology – and always believed he was doing the right thing, both for his business and for the nation.

He now recognizes the problem of over-production in most basic commodities. He accepts that it is in the national interest to contain this over-production and 'rein in' a system 'which has slightly overrun its target', but in doing so he feels that it is important that this should not prejudice Britain's capacity to remain self-sufficient in food. He fears a 'repeat of the repeal of the Corn Laws' when domestic production was deliberately run down and imports were allowed to affect the home farming economy adversely. His preferred solution is to continue the drive towards efficient production, recognizing that this will have serious consequences for the structure of the industry. The inefficient farmer will go out of business and there will be an inevitable decline in the number of farmers remaining. He intends to ensure that his own business is in a position to compete and survive.

John Kerr's optimism depends partly on a confidence in his own management (as opposed to farming) skills and partly on the location and quality of the farm's own resources. For example, he continues to see a future in dairy production because the bulk of his farm's milk goes into liquid consumption. Since he is only 80 miles from the only capital city in the world with a daily milk delivery, he suspects that his milk will still be in demand after others have ceased production. His vegetables are supplied to the market leader in frozen foods, his barley finds its way into malt that goes into beer and lager, his poultry into processed cuts which can be found in any supermarket, and so on. In other words, the Kerrs' production, at least, is not sold into storage, but ends up on supermarket shelves.

He recognizes the need, however, to take a cool look at the resources of his business and to be prepared to diversify into other profitable areas. Already he is responsible for a leisure enterprise (a farm park, established by his brother) and a management consultancy. But he is sceptical whether all farmers can move in this direction – or should. Part-time farming might be the answer for those who are unable or unwilling to keep their place on the farming treadmill. He recognizes the social problem which the small farmer represents, but can see no alternative to allowing normal competitive forces to hold sway.

——— CHARLES OWSTON ———

It is a long way – and not just in miles – from the fertile loams and clays of Suffolk to the harsh conditions of the Cumbrian fells. At Bewcastle, north-east of Carlisle, Charles Owston farms 134 acres of fellside, plus a share of the common land on top of the fell, at an altitude rising from 700 to 1100 feet above sea level. He bought the farm in 1972, after a career as a research scientist. He and his wife Judith, a local farmer's daughter, farm 280 breeding ewes and 19 geese. They let summer grazing for 35 cattle.

For most of this century farming here has been a struggle. Small though the farm is by comparison with John Kerr's it incorporates one other holding, its farmhouse now derelict, last occupied in 1935. When Charles and Judith Owston arrived the newest building on the farm was a barn which had been erected in 1906. In the early 1970s the Owstons found that they had on their hands what was essentially an 1890s' farmstead – and a small cottage furnished to Edwardian standards of domestic comfort.

The land had been poorly managed. The whole farm was exceedingly acid, even though the land was basically sound and dry. Indeed the visible signs of ploughed terraces show that cereals had once been grown for the horses and for domestic consumption! Although it was impossible to plough out and re-seed the land Charles Owston nevertheless set about improving it through the successive application of lime and phosphate. He erected new farm buildings, whose convenience allowed the farm to be run by one person. He also began to produce more of his own hay for winter feed – not an easy task because the high humidity makes it difficult to dry. Such investment could only be worthwhile if production could be expanded; similarly production could only be expanded if investment was made. Charles, too, obeyed government exhortations to expand production. He built a new cattle barn, borrowing the money to pay for it. Now it stands empty: beef production no longer pays.

The trade in sheep is better, but this kind of farmer is at the sharp end of the 'cost–price squeeze'. The price of his fat sheep has risen by 50 per cent in twelve years, while costs have more than doubled. His solution has been to intensify as far as possible, but nevertheless the margin which the Owstons have to live on is declining all the time. As Charles points out, the plight of the hill farmer does not manifest itself through some sudden and obvious calamity which signals an irretrievable end to the business. Instead it is a kind of creeping paralysis, the steady drip, drip of increasing difficulty. There is always the hope that a bad year will be succeeded by one that is better. But farming here is a survival against the odds.

UPLAND FARMING IS VERY MUCH A FAMILY AFFAIR.
JUDITH OWSTON – WITH SOME HELP FROM 18-MONTH-OLD
JEREMY – PROVIDES LUNCH FOR THE GEESE FLOCK

As a hill farmer Charles Owston receives subsidies on his sheep. To use EEC parlance his farm is in a Less Favoured Area. In practice, however, LFA payments barely affect the squeeze on his margins. At the end of the day the future depends on what Charles and Judith will accept for an income. They have four chilldren and, not unreasonably, seek a standard of living which the rest of the population has come to expect. There are limits to the frugality they can be asked to bear. Currently the Owstons' farming income is less than that of John Kerr's tractor drivers. They do not farm for the money, but for the pride and satisfaction they obtain from doing a hard job well. But there is a bottom line.

They are understandably worried about the future. The resources of the farm do not lend themselves to setting up ancillary enterprises. They let a caravan for holiday-makers, but there is not much of a tourist trade in this part of the world. Their farm is on a spectacularly beautiful site, but to reach it requires a determined effort to negotiate twisty lanes, cross moors and fell and climb up a difficult gated track from the nearest road. The effort is well worthwhile, but there is no casual passing trade and the summer season up here is short – little more than three months. Whatever attempts are made to diversify farming here will remain hopelessly uneconomic in narrow accounting terms. But if farmers like the Owstons are allowed to go out of production, the impact on the uplands would be considerable. Parishes like Bewcastle, founded by the Romans, would struggle to survive as viable communities. The landscape of the mountains and fells – very much a product of the way farmers like the Owstons manage their land – would revert to disfiguring scrub and derelict buildings. Most likely the Owstons' farm would disappear under conifer trees – already the edge of Kielder Forest, the largest man-made forest in Europe, looms broodingly on the horizon above their farm.

HYWEL BROWN

The structure of British farming is a spectrum which runs from farms like the Kerrs to those like the Owstons. But traditionally the backbone of British farming has been represented by those like Hywel Brown: the medium-sized family farm. Like many family farmers Hywel Brown specializes in dairy production. He farms just over 100 acres – less than the Owstons but on much more fertile land – near Narberth in what was Pembrokeshire and is now Dyfed. He has 62 dairy cows and a beef herd of 35. His father farmed here since 1947 and Hywel took over the farm in 1964. He and his wife Sheila have two sons, the oldest of whom, Gethin, also works on the farm.

The Browns are the modern embodiment of rural Britain's traditional yeoman qualities. It is farmers like these who are responsible for much of the regional diversity – the 'patchwork quilt' – of the British countryside. They epitomize the hard work and bluff common sense we associate with John Bull – or Dan Archer. For Hywel Brown farming, to use the familiar cliché, is not just a business, but a way of life. There is no real distinction between home and work, and the farm bears all the signs of personal care and attention which go well beyond what is economically necessary. Hywel possesses a strong desire to retain the farm within the family – 'to keep the name on the land' – and to enable his son to succeed to a farm which is viable and in good heart.

THE MODERN EMBODIMENT OF RURAL BRITAIN'S TRADITIONAL YEOMAN QUALITIES:
HYWEL BROWN AND HIS SON GETHIN

Like other dairy farmers Hywel Brown paid attention to the need to expand his production and improve his efficiency. Over the years he has improved his land, expanded the size of his herd, invested in new buildings and equipment and modernized his farming operations. In common with other medium-sized family farmers he has sometimes felt ambivalent about this, but he really had no alternative. Family farmers are sometimes pushed only reluctantly into the harsher commercial world of finance, credit, cost-accounting and the other necessities of obtaining the maximum return on capital investment. But in order to maintain an equitable standard of living for his family he has had little choice. By manipulating the levers of control which affect costs and prices government policy has encouraged farmers like Hywel Brown to acquire at least some of the attitudes of John Kerr. The alternative has been to join the annual struggle for survival on the margins of the industry.

So Hywel Brown expanded and modernized and looked forward to reaping the rewards which Ministers of Agriculture had held out for him. But Hywel is a dairy farmer and dairy farming, more than any other section of the farming industry, has recently suffered from the vicissitudes of policy-makers. Hywel, like others, discovered that government policy statements can be fickle friends. Towards the end of 1983 a long-heralded budgetary crisis in the CAP duly arrived. The level of price supports had risen to such dizzy heights as to reach the expenditure limits laid down by the member states of the EEC. The budgetary crisis provoked a political crisis, with the British government taking the lead in refusing to sanction an increase in expenditure without a thorough structural reform of the CAP, a reform which would reduce surpluses and hence public expenditure. By 1984 the Thatcher administration was engaged in a costly dispute in the coalmining industry, where the central issue was the level of support to be given to high-cost pits producing coal which the market could not absorb. There were some obvious parallels with agriculture – and it was difficult to make a stand against the miners while allowing the CAP to spiral out of control.

Radical change was therefore predictable, but the form it took was not. Hywel Brown expected some tightening up of margins on milk production in order to discourage further expansion. In the event an entirely different and novel mechanism was used: production quotas. With considerable swiftness and severity the dairy sector was subjected to a physical reduction on the amount of milk it could produce – with, in effect, fines for over-production. Quotas were effective but crude: Hywel Brown, who had been encouraged to expand and was locked into a lengthy production cycle, was faced with an immediate loss of income. Existing production could not be sustained without

him being penalized; similarly a reduction in his herd would produce a decline in profit unless something could be done to reduce costs disproportionately.

Not surprisingly Hywel Brown feels bitter. He has been beaten over the head with the nearest blunt instrument which came to hand. He has reacted in the conventional farming manner: tightened his belt and become resigned to sitting it out. Other farmers in his area have been less fortunate. Those who financed their earlier expansion on the basis of increased borrowings are in dire straits. Their falling incomes have made it difficult, or even impossible, to service their loans. Declining returns have led to a fall in the value of farm land – the very land that has been used as collateral for the loans. Foreclosures by the banks have become commonplace. The roadsides of Pembrokeshire are festooned with 'For Sale' signs. But there are few local buyers. A 250-acre dairy farm, with quota, can be purchased for the price of a four-bedroom detached house in the Home Counties. Smart yuppie money is moving in. But a farming community is being destroyed.

Hywel Brown is not afraid of change and he would be the first to agree that the taxpayer does not owe him a living. What he asks for is a clear, and above all consistent set of policy signals which will enable him to plan ahead. Farm production cannot be turned on and off like a tap. Often the most precious commodity to a dairy farmer is time. There are few signs, however, that a carefully thought-out strategy for the future of British farming is being constructed, nor is Hywel Brown confident that a consistent set of goals will replace those set for farmers in the late 1940s. At present the family farmer does not know where to turn or what is expected of him. The public, it is believed, either does not know or does not care about the future of farming.

FARMING IN THE FUTURE

Each of these three farmers has been influenced by four decades of technological change and agricultural policy – but in clearly divergent ways. Strategic policy decisions taken now will determine their survival chances up until the twenty-first century. As a nation we will then have wished upon ourselves the kind of farming industry we deserve.

For example, agricultural productivity has now progressed to the point where we could meet most of our food needs by encouraging the further expansion of farmers like John Kerr and winding down public support for the remainder. In the wake of such a decision both the character of our rural communities and the ecology and

THE PATCHWORK QUILT OF THE BRITISH COUNTRYSIDE:
PORLOCK VALE, DORSET. MUCH OF THE ATTRACTIVENESS
OF THE BRITISH COUNTRYSIDE LIES IN THE CLOSE HARMONY
BETWEEN THE DIFFERENT ELEMENTS OF THE LANDSCAPE.
HERE OPEN HEATHER MOORLAND IS SIDE BY SIDE WITH
INTENSIVE ARABLE CULTIVATION. IT IS IMPORTANT THAT
SUCH DIVERSITY IS RETAINED IN THE FUTURE

landscape of the countryside would change – whether for the better or worse is a matter of judgement, but certainly in ways which would need to be taken into account. The concentration of resources on fewer farms would also release land for other uses. Estimates vary, but it has been calculated that up to 10 million acres – an area the size of Devon and Derbyshire combined – could be taken out of agricultural production by the 1990s. Figures like these have concentrated policy-makers' minds on the scale of impending change. But there is little consensus over what to do – and the public, which might be supposed to have an interest in such matters, is scarcely aware of what is in store. Among the options being canvassed are the following:

• *A general reduction in the level of support.* In keeping with the spirit of the times this would open up farming to free market forces by engineering a decline in prices to close to world levels. If this were to be coupled with a retention of the Less Favoured Areas as a safety net for hill farmers, the casualties would be neither the agribusinessmen (big enough and, probably, efficient enough to survive) nor the small farmer (who is flexible, thrifty and can rely on low-cost family labour), but the middle-sized farmers, especially those who have borrowed to expand. The result would be a further shift towards a dual farming structure, and a decimation of farming in areas like the Midlands and the West Country. In any case it has proved, so far, politically impossible to find agreement on this within the EEC where few governments can contemplate the political consequences of driving the (much more numerous) 'inefficient' producers out of business. Only if the CAP is 're-nationalized' (by no means impossible) could Britain go it alone on this. One further problem is that farmers might compensate for the squeeze on returns by producing still more – and creating even larger surpluses!

• *Target support on the efficient farmers.* Essentially a variant on the above. Through a combination of threats and inducements small farmers would be encouraged to leave the industry while the agribusinessman would be given further incentives to expand and invest. It all depends on what one means by 'efficient', of course. Many large-scale farms are only efficient in relation to their costs (crop yields per acre, etc. are frequently *lower* on larger farms), so it is possible to render large farms inefficient at a stroke, as it were, by tinkering with the cost structure – for example, increase the cost of oil, tax fertilizers, subsidized labour, etc. In any case what would happen to the small farmer is not altogether clear (see below).

• *Encourage lower input farming.* Under this option the same amount of land would be used, but it would be farmed less intensively. Yields might fall, but so would costs, and profits would be sustained. In this way surpluses could be reduced by a deliberate

decision to put the clock back on technological progress. In practice this would not be too cataclysmic – combine harvesters would not exactly rust away in the corners of farmyards – but there would be less use of chemicals, a move back towards mixed farming systems and, perhaps, more use of labour. This option is much favoured by environmental groups and those concerned about the over-use of chemicals, but there are powerful industrial interests lined up against it, and both farmers and policy-makers are suspicious of its practicability.

• *'Set-aside'*. A current ministry favourite, this involves paying farmers to keep land out of production. To make real inroads into the surpluses it would have to be applied disproportionately to the *most* productive farmers. Estimates suggest that as much as one-third of cereals land would have to lie fallow. This poses an intriguing public relations problem: how to convince a sceptical taxpayer that large amounts of money should be paid to already well-off farmers to do nothing. The system would also have to be policed in order to prevent cheating – the day-to-day interference in farming operations could be quite extensive. One added difficulty is that historical experience suggests that it will not work. The United States has a long and sorry history of set-aside; in the 1970s a 30 per cent reduction in the land used for corn resulted in a 3 per cent increase in output! Farmers simply took their worst land out of production and farmed the remainder more intensively, while gratefully pocketing large amounts of federal dollars. Its popularity in influential circles in Britain mystifies most outside observers.

• *Encourage part-time farming*. In continental Europe it is common for a large proportion of farmers to be part time. In Britain, although the proportion is higher than generally acknowledged, there is no recognition of part-time farming as a desirable status. Indeed the Ministry of Agriculture has long assumed that a part-time farmer is a stage along the road to becoming an ex-farmer and they have not been eligible for support. If part-time farming were to be encouraged, however, the claims on the exchequer for support might be reduced, since many might settle for less than a full-time income. There might even be many people who would *like* to become part-time farmers. But fears of recreating a British peasantry and nineteenth-century folk memories of 'three acres and a cow' present severe obstacles to the idea being considered seriously.

• *Diversification*. Like 'set-aside' this is currently a buzz-word in policy circles. It can be interpreted in two ways. The first involves switching production from commod-ities which are in surplus to those which could usefully be expanded. There are few

LOWER INPUT FARMING: SIGHTS LIKE THIS MIGHT BECOME MORE COMMON

immediately obvious candidates, though a good deal of scientific endeavour has been directed towards finding them. Near-misses include sunflowers, lupins and evening primroses (all for use in vegetable oil), while more bizarre offerings have from time to time been canvassed. Already there is some diversification in areas which exploit new markets: goats' milk and cheese; specialist wool production from goats, rabbits, llamas and rare breeds of sheep; venison farming, trout farming, etc. The second sense of diversification is to use the resources of the farm for things other than agriculture. Since early 1987 farmers have been encouraged via the Alternative Land Use and Rural Enterprise (ALURE) package to seek assistance for on-farm tourism, conversions of redundant farm buildings, and so on. There are well-publicized examples of farms turned into golf courses, theme parks, holiday centres, small business estates and a myriad other alternatives (some of which are examined in Chapter 7). Again the intention is both to supplement falling farm incomes and, in some cases, take land out of production. By no means all farmers have the opportunity to participate, however, because of the location and character of their holdings.

• *Afforestation.* In some respects this can be seen as a special kind of diversification. Britain imports 92 per cent of its timber. Therefore, the argument runs, land should be taken out of agricultural production and planted over with trees. In the past

afforestation has meant the notorious mass planting of conifers, often much detested for their impact on the landscape and wildlife. Large-scale forestry interests would certainly like to come down from the mountains to the valley floors where more fertile land could produce quicker returns. But there is an increasing move towards more 'viewer-friendly' forestry: encouraging farmers to use land for small-scale plantations of both hard and softwoods – or 'agri-forestry' as it is known. Many farmers, unfortunately, lack the requisite skills and returns are uncertain, but this option is one which could receive considerable backing.

• *Conservation*. Some of the above options would clearly have an impact on the quality of the rural environment, but arguments have also been put forward to switch a proportion of support from production to environmental conservation – in other words pay farmers to achieve a desired environmental outcome. A small step has already been taken in this direction via the designation of Environmentally Sensitive Areas (ESAs) where farmers are entitled to payments which help to achieve desired environmental objectives (see Chapters 4 and 5). The scheme has met some resistance from farmers (who have objected to being considered 'glorified park wardens') but initial experience has, on the whole, been encouraging. This is a scheme aimed primarily at conservation and not at the problem of reducing surpluses, however. Nevertheless some conservationists would like to see large tracts of land being allowed to revert to wilderness areas. How the population in such areas might view this prospect has not been recorded.

• *Recreation*. The whole issue of recreation and public access o the countryside is taken up in Chapter 6. Here it is only necessary to note that the release of land from farming, or the introduction of less intensive farming methods, will provide new opportunities for recreation and leisure in the countryside. Many farmers are already taking advantage of this.

• *Development*. Since the war we have become so accustomed to believing that every acre must be preciously guarded for agriculture that it takes a considerable leap of the imagination to realize what could be done with 10 million acres made available for housing and industrial development. It has to be stated immediately that even in their wildest dreams Barrett's, Wimpey's, *et al.* would not envisage laying claim to development land of this magnitude. And yet . . . a number of options relating to the development of cities, industrial relocation, new towns and other forms of development could become available. Planning restrictions on rural development, even in Green Belts, appear *prima facie* to be more difficult to justify as a result.

These are some of the alternatives now being considered. It is unlikely that any one of them will be pursued to the exclusion of all the others. Much more likely is some kind of mix – but in what proportion? Overshadowing all of this is the question, what is the role of farming to be in the countryside of the future? In the past, as we have seen, the role of farming was clear – to produce more and cheaper food. As a nation we had to learn how to manage an era of unprecedented agricultural expansion. Now we are having to learn how to manage a decline – and the transition is not proving to be easy.

We are having to face up to the fact that farming in the future may not be devoted exclusively to producing food. In some areas public support for agriculture may be granted because it conserves wildlife, because it maintains a cherished landscape, because it forms the basis of the local economy and rural community, because it provides a setting for recreation and tourism – or for a combination of all these reasons. If so, the *kind* of farming that is encouraged may be at some variance from agriculture which is exclusively production-oriented.

The production of food has dominated the history of the countryside. It will remain important in the countryside of the future. But the countryside will no longer be synonymous with farming, nor farming with the production of food. It is no exaggeration to say that we have reached a turning-point in our rural development. Agriculture may have been responsible for the changing countryside in the past, but today rural Britain is subject to a much more complex series of changes. As the next chapter shows, when we come to consider the people who inhabit the countryside, then the changes have been dramatic indeed.

EFFICIENT, HI-TECH PRODUCTION – BUT FOR HOW MUCH LONGER?
BRINGING IN THE HARVEST ON THE DOWNS IN OXFORDSHIRE

CHANGE IN THE VILLAGE

THE COUNTRY VILLAGE HAS always had a special place in our affections. To many of us it represents the ideal community. We take it for granted that village life provokes a sense of neighbourliness and friendship – a sense of belonging. Village life seems to proceed at its own pace, with its own priorities, undisturbed by the upheavals of war, politics and the modern urban rat-race. The timbered cottage and quaint country pub, clustered around the ancient church and village green, summarize our rural heritage.

As a result most of us feel that the rural village is a real community in a way in which, say, a suburban housing estate can never be. Here, surely, we can put down some roots. But the reality is that village life has always been rooted in the local rural economy and just as the economy of the countryside has been changing rapidly, so too has life in the village.

We like to look upon village life as timeless and unchanging, but historians have shown that this is far from being true. Even the buildings and the layout of the village are usually quite recent in their development – not much older than the towns and cities which we often feel have a much shorter history. In the lowland areas of the south and east of Britain, for example, the characteristic village – closely clustered together around the church or manor house – is a product of the Agricultural Revolution of the late eighteenth century and the enclosure movement which accompanied it. At this time farmsteads and dwellings, which had previously been scattered across the countryside, gravitated towards a recognizable village centre. Later, during Victorian times when agriculture enjoyed considerable prosperity, farmers left the village to live in what were often newly-built farmhouses located away from the village centre on their own holdings of land.

In lowland areas, then, only the church, the manor house and a few cottages pre-date the nineteenth century. Those villages which can claim a longer period of undisturbed history were usually not villages at all, but medieval textile towns which were 'de-industrialized' during the Industrial Revolution. Today's examples of spectacular Cotswold or Suffolk villages, for example, lost out to the industrial north of England during the nineteenth century and slid back into a dependency on agriculture. The thousands of visitors who each year throng places like Lavenham, Broadway or Castle Combe are perhaps unaware that they have been subject to successive periods of change which their ancient appearance somewhat belies.

In the upland areas of the north and west of Britan, however, we can still find a very different pattern of settlement. Historically, the pastoral economy of the uplands – based on the rearing of animals, rather than on the tending of crops – allowed the old medieval pattern of scattered farmsteads to continue. Villages were – and, to some extent, are – less common. Settlement in each parish was much more dispersed and in many areas a pattern of scattered hamlets and small market towns predominated. Even here, though, settlement is much more recent than is sometimes supposed. Remoter areas, like Cumbria for example, were still being colonized as late as the eighteenth century, while other areas, most notoriously the Scottish highlands, were being depopulated on a large scale to make way for sheep. So, then, as a whole, rural settlements are neither as immemorial nor as unchanging as is sometimes believed. The only unchanging feature has been change itself.

SETTLEMENT PATTERNS IN UPLAND AREAS ARE MORE SCATTERED: NIDDERDALE, YORKS

—— THE VILLAGE – YESTERDAY AND TODAY ——

Village communities pride themselves on their own distinctive qualities. It is true that in many respects no two villages are alike. But one generalization which can be made is that historically the village was above all a *working* community and that for most villages, especially from the nineteenth century onwards, this work was farming. Of course, this was never completely the case – there remained examples of rural villages where the economic basis was not agriculture but some other industry, such as mining, quarrying, fishing, craft manufacture and so on. But once the Industrial Revolution had centred manufacturing on towns and cities, agriculture dominated the economy of the countryside and therefore the life of most villages.

This meant that the character of the village varied considerably according to the kind of local farming economy, not only between the pastoral uplands and the arable lowlands, but also between those villages which were under the sway of a large local estate and those granted a more independent existence. At the end of the nineteenth century large estates covered over one-quarter of the surface area of Britain. Estate villages were known as 'closed' villages (mainly because it was more difficult to obtain housing in them). At their centre lay the 'big house' with its imposing architectural presence, its parkland and gardens and its extensive retinue of servants and other domestic workers. Aristocratic grandees could run the village as a local fiefdom – and many did. But for many village inhabitants there were also advantages to be gained from the protection which the big house offered from the worst aspects of poverty and insecurity. In the 'open' villages the more egalitarian tenor of life was mitigated by insecure employment and slum housing conditions which were the scandal of late Victorian times. Some villages, indeed, received widespread notoriety as centres of moral iniquity and hotbeds of social unrest.

Whatever their moral and social character, however, the population of most rural villages remained dependent upon agriculture for its living. Even those villagers not working directly on the land would usually be involved in occupations closely associated with farming, such as blacksmiths, wheelwrights and millers. The typical village was a truly agricultural community. Often village neighbours were also workmates – and even kin. The life of the village was forged out of a common experience of both work *and* leisure. Codes of behaviour could be enforced through family ties and a widespread knowledge of everyone's business. No wonder that strangers could find village life almost impenetrable.

As with any isolated and largely self-contained community the agricultural village was often the subject of a fierce loyalty among its inhabitants. From their own customs and traditions the villagers could draw upon a strong sense of their own identity and standing. It gave the village a collective strength in times of adversity; but the ambitious, the rebellious, or simply the single-minded, could find the village a narrow-minded and mean-spirited prison. Village gossip could be a cruel weapon. The close-knit village could be both a welcoming haven from a cruel world and a dispiriting internment camp where boredom vied with boorishness.

There was often a sharp division between the 'official' and 'unofficial' village community, especially in estate villages. The official community was led, inevitably, by the Big House, whose members attended the church, patronized the local tradesmen and supervised the affairs of the village. They felt entitled to, and duly received, the customary deference that was accorded to their rank. They led the official community life of the village in the annual round of village customs and festivals and in sports as diverse as cricket and foxhunting the official village celebrated its own sense of community. The unofficial village, though, was a rather different affair – often directly opposed to, but hidden from, the local landowners. It contained its own thriving rural underworld which revolved around the four-ale bar and the poaching gang, a world of cock-fighting and bull-baiting, a world where a rather different moral order prevailed.

Prestige in the village community did not necessarily coincide with the more obvious rankings of income and wealth. As a working community the village often reserved its greatest respect for those who possessed the greatest skill in their work. The devoted stockman or the skilled ploughman were often granted the highest status. Much of their handiwork was available for public inspection. It was quite common to see groups of farm workers walking around country lanes on Sunday mornings, peering over the hedgerows in order to inspect each other's ploughing. Claims which had been made in the bar during the week were solemnly adjudicated. A botched piece of ploughing or drilling was not only visible for all to see, but would remain so for several weeks. Similar evaluations were made and exchanged over the skills of shepherds and stockmen at local markets and shows. The public at large may have regarded those working in agriculture as unskilled yokels, but the village knew better. And it was the opinion of the village which mattered.

Of course the village was never completely isolated from the outside world. The business of earning a living – of trade and commerce and markets – ensured that. But

towards the end of the nineteenth century the relative isolation of village life began to be broken down. By the 1880s most villages had reasonable access to the railway system, bringing in cheaper coal and manufactured goods and allowing rural inhabitants to begin buying consumer goods already available in towns. The railways also distributed national daily newspapers. New ideas, new tastes, new lifestyles began to invade the traditional pattern of rural life.

From this time on the pace of change quickened remarkably. Today the village is no longer – except in a few remote areas – an agricultural community. It has been transformed both by changes within agriculture – most notably the massive decrease in farm labour consequent upon mechanization – and by changes from outside – especially developments in transport which have allowed an entirely new village population to move in. This process began between the wars. The depression had produced a marked decline in the rural population as those working on the land migrated, or even emigrated, in search of employment, but at this time the countryside was 'discovered' as a desirable place not only to visit but in which to live, especially in the Home Counties around London. Commuting was promoted, sometimes jointly, by railway companies and speculative builders. The best-known example, remembered through its vivid advertising and the poems of John Betjeman, was 'Metroland', the string of commuting villages developed along the extension of the Metropolitan Railway north-westwards from London, to Aylesbury and beyond. Posters and hoardings beckoned prospective buyers of mock-Tudor villas to 'pleasing prospects' less than an hour from Baker Street.

After the Second World War these changes became much more widespread. Farm mechanization was producing a large surplus of workers on the land; the booming post-war economy sucked them into jobs in urban areas. Meanwhile, widespread car ownership allowed a new race of villager to replace them. The social changes which first became apparent in the Home Counties spread like a series of waves out along the roads, railway lines and, later, motorways to cover virtually the whole of rural Britain. Suddenly, so it seemed to many local people, the village had been transformed from an agricultural community into a commuter dormitory, a retirement centre or a weekend retreat. Whatever it was, it was no longer based on farming.

The irony is that it was the farming industry itself which set these changes in motion. The technological changes which were discussed in the last chapter brought social changes in their wake. As the agricultural population was displaced, so it moved

out, to be replaced by an urban, overwhelmingly middle-class population, which was attracted in by a combination of cheap housing (until prices moved swiftly upwards after the late 1960s) and their idyllic vision of life in a real community. This legion of newcomers to rural life was able, thanks to the car and the railway, to indulge its romantic vision of life in a country cottage – while still enjoying the material benefits which modern urban life had to offer.

Today motorways have linked up most of the commuting areas between the major cities and the in-filling of commuter villages between these radial transport routes has virtually been completed. Thanks to the motorway and the Inter-City 125, whole tracts of hitherto rural areas like the West Country have become outer suburbs of London. Only a few places, isolated by bad roads and non-existent railways, remain relatively untouched, but even these, by virtue of their isolation, have become susceptible to the equally voracious demand for holiday homes and weekend cottages. Rural Britain, once agricultural Britain, has thus become urban, middle-class Britain.

The new 'immigrants' have brought with them lifestyles largely alien to the remaining local, agricultural population. Unlike the locals, the newcomers do not necessarily make the village the focus of all their social activities since their possession of a car allows them to continue to make use of urban services and amenities. So this influx of outsiders quite rapidly changes the nature of village society. Suddenly, so it seems, everybody does *not* know everybody else. New social divisions arise – typically between the closely-knit locals, increasingly enclaved on the council estate and among the agricultural tied cottages, and the ex-urban newcomers, affluent, by no means wholly insensitive, but nevertheless disruptive of established ways.

The sense of loss for the locals can be quite severe. Faced with an invasion of 'their' community by townie outsiders their resentment has grown. For example, many newcomers arrive full of goodwill and good intentions, but fail to recognize the disruption they cause. Some regard farm workers as unskilled labourers – and, worse still, *call* them farm labourers, a term most farm workers loathe. Newcomers simply lack the knowledge of farming skills to appreciate what is involved. They certainly do not drive around the lanes on Sunday morning inspecting the ploughing. Their judgements are not based on malice, but on established urban criteria for assessing the worth of others – mainly the visible signs of affluence like the house, the car, consumer durables, and so on. In this league many low-paid villagers will be assigned a place close to the bottom.

IN MOST VILLAGES IN BRITAIN THE LOCAL, AGRICULTURAL
POPULATION IS INCREASINGLY CONFINED TO THE RENTED SECTOR.
COUNCIL HOUSES IN SHILTON, OXFORDSHIRE

BALANCED COMMUNITY DEVELOPMENT NEED NOT BE
INCOMPATIBLE WITH THE RETENTION OF TRANQUILLITY:
ARDINGTON, OXFORDSHIRE

Even an over-sensitive desire to retain the goodwill of the locals may create problems. Many newcomers value the presence of the farming population, if only because it serves as a reminder that the village remains truly rural rather than a kind of rustic suburbia. But the locals can be assigned a definite place in the scheme of things. They can be 'characters', sources of quaint bucolic humour or homespun rural philosophy on such matters as the seasons or the weather, but not expected to put forward views which intrude on the newcomer's sense of how things should be done. What are demanded are pet locals who adorn the landscape along with the fields and the trees.

Inevitably conflicts arise from time to time. Threatened by a loss of status in their own village, the locals frequently change the rules of the competition. They base social acceptance not on the visible signs of affluence, but on length of residence. In this way they can retain their former position among those who share their judgements. Soon newcomers begin to grumble about not being accepted until they have three generations buried in the churchyard and glumly resign themselves to thirty years' residence before they will become 'part of the village'. In the pub the locals drink in the public bar, while the newcomers patronize the lounge, often modernized in a recherché rustic decor for their benefit.

The clash of two cultures may also be observed at the village fête. Newcomers tend to concentrate on the wine-making and the flower-arranging; the locals divide their time between the beer tent and the equally serious business of the fruit and vegetable show, a forum in which their skills are still subject to public competition. For those newcomers who have sought the happy intimacy of rural life, the reserve (and worse) of the locals can be mystifying. But all too often the village is now two social worlds divided by common residence.

Sometimes the mutual misunderstanding of locals and newcomers has its amusing side. But underlying the common incomprehension of alien ways of life there are often more serious matters at stake. Principal among these is housing. It is something over which the entire rural population – locals and newcomers – competes. Newcomers have contributed to the increasing demand for rural housing, pricing it out of the range of most locals who are on lower incomes. Similar conditions apply to privately-rented housing – letting for holiday-makers is frequently more lucrative. Resentment among local people has grown at their inability to find local housing for themselves and their children. They have also found that newcomers frequently oppose the construction of new housing, especially council housing, on the grounds that it is 'detrimental to the character of the village'.

Indeed newcomers often oppose *any* change, including both housing and commercial development, even where, in the judgement of the locals, it is necessary for the continued well-being of the village. Articulate and influential, the newcomers have been able to ensure that local planning policies reflect their point of view. They operate what might be termed the 'drawbridge effect': having made it into their rural idyll, they wish to keep the village, as they would see it, unspoiled. Such attitudes are most common in the south of England where there are now powerful local political forces lined up against any form of village growth. Given half the chance they would designate virtually all of the countryside as Green Belt and veto any form of development.

Such changes mean that a whole new social balance now underpins village life. In many, if not most, villages it is the newcomers who are now in the majority and they who influence the future shape of village development. The locals can find, somewhat disconcertingly, that their needs are overlooked. This applies particularly to those who are vulnerable to any decrease in the provision of local services, especially transport. The poor, the elderly and the disabled cannot step into their cars and drive to the nearest urban centre to take advantage of a full range of services and amenities. At the same time the affluent majority is often unable or unwilling to foot the rapidly-rising bill for public service provision.

In many areas what has emerged is an alarming degree of social polarization, involving not only subjective differences in lifestyles, but actual living standards, between those who have chosen to live in the countryside and those who have been stranded there by decades of social and economic change over which they have had no control. Two nations in one village has increasingly become the norm.

Rural deprivation is not new. But in the past poverty was an experience shared by most of the village. Now it brings only a sense of exclusion. Many of the poorer sections of the village community are trapped by a lack of access to housing, alternative employment and the full range of amenities which their more affluent neighbours take for granted. A way of life once only distantly and fleetingly observed is now frequently encountered at first hand among the new inhabitants of 'their' village. They have found that their needs go unacknowledged. Their minority status hardly lends itself to making a fuss, nor to the expectation that they could achieve any tangible change if they attempted to do so. Generations of inherited experience form an accurate guide here. Instead, like their predecessors when contemplating their local squire, they mostly grumble and 'make do'.

PLANNING POLICIES HAVE BEEN DISPROPORTIONATELY CONCERNED
WITH THE PHYSICAL APPEARANCE OF OUR VILLAGES.
THIS IS AN UNDERSTANDABLE RESPONSE TO AN EARLIER ERA
WHEN 'RIBBON DEVELOPMENT' WAS PREVALENT.
NEAR HOWARTH, WEST YORKSHIRE MODERN HOUSING STRAGGLES
DOWN THE HILLSIDE AWAY FROM THE HISTORIC VILLAGE CORE

—— A TALE OF TWO VILLAGES ——

Have we seen the end of the village as a real community? Certainly we have seen the end of the village as an agricultural community. It has been the disruption accompanying this process which accounts for much of the friction between locals and newcomers. Have newcomers, then, destroyed the village community – or have they revitalized the village which would otherwise have died on its feet? The experiences of two very different villages, in different parts of the country, may help to provide some clues to the answers.

—— SHILTON ——

On first encounter Shilton seems to come straight off the lid of a chocolate box. It is a picture postcard English village, situated on the edge of the Cotswolds, 20 miles west of Oxford on a tributary of the river Windrush. It is tucked away off a main road in a shallow valley. The village is almost entirely built from Cotswold stone. The cottages straggle along the single main street, at the centre of which lies a shallow and slowly-moving river crossed by a ford accompanied by a low packhorse bridge. On a summer's day the village basks in mellow sunshine, gardens ablaze with flowers, the peace and tranquillity disturbed only by the occasional aircraft from nearby RAF Brize Norton. Even by the exquisite standards of the Cotswolds Shilton is a beautiful place.

The attractiveness of Shilton makes it much sought after as a village in which to live. Its location is also convenient. The city of Oxford can be reached in less than half an hour; London, thanks to the construction of the M40 motorway, is within commuting distance. Shilton is also favoured as a weekend retreat. But Shilton's beauty has led to its designation as a conservation area. There are no new houses to speak of in Shilton: these have been constructed in the distinctly unattractive village of Carterton nearby. So a house in Shilton is at a premium. Increasing demand has not been met by an expansion in supply. And as house prices have gone up, so Shilton has become more and more socially exclusive.

On a midweek afternoon Shilton slumbers. It is very quiet, almost deserted. This is because the majority of its inhabitants are not there. They are away in Oxford or London. So Shilton by day is almost a ghost village. The manicured gardens, the tastefully restored cottages take on a slight air of unreality. Shilton is like a Doctor Dolittle film set from which the crew have taken a break.

It was not always like this. Shilton once had five farmyards in the centre of the

SHILTON WAS ONCE AN AGRICULTURAL COMMUNITY. . .

SHILTON VILLAGE
CENTRE AT THE TURN
OF THE CENTURY

village, complete with pigs and cattle. Virtually all the cottages in Shilton were lived in by farm workers and their families. The village had a full range of amenities until well after the Second World War: church, chapel, school, post office, shops, pub, football team, cricket team – all at that time utterly unremarkable. Shilton had its own baker, its hurdle-maker and its blacksmith. There were always people gathered around the forge exchanging gossip and passing the time of day. Indeed older residents remember Shilton as a busy pace. People were 'sort of everywhere and you knew them all'. There were constant comings and goings from the farms and in the afternoon the children – up to fifty at one time – would leave school and head for home, shouting and running in the street, pausing at the blacksmith's shop or the fish pond. In the evenings the older men would gather at the corners; others would head for the allotments, returning with their bicycles laden with vegetables. At almost any time of day it was impossible to walk through Shilton without having to pause and pass the time of day chatting to a neighbour, relative or workmate.

In two short decades from the 1950s onwards nearly all of this was swept away. Shilton, like similar villages up and down the country, began to feel the effects of agricultural change. Machines replaced men and former farm workers began to leave the village to find employment in nearby towns. The smaller farms in the area were bought up by the larger ones. New farming methods removed the need for a hurdle-maker and a blacksmith. Bit by bit the old agricultural community began to fade away.

SHILTON VILLAGE CENTRE TODAY

THE ROSE AND CROWN, SHILTON,
AT THE TURN OF THE CENTURY

Shilton itself did not die, but it was transformed. A different kind of person began to move in: retired air force officers, bank managers, university professors, architects, film producers, company directors – a varied range of professional and managerial people whose work was often based as far away as London. They busily set about converting what were often somewhat dilapidated farm workers' cottages into highly desirable residences, sometimes knocking two or three former houses into one for the purpose. Even the barns which were attached to the former farm buildings in the village centre were converted to houses. The last remaining barn in the village has recently been sold off to provide a home for an 'in-comer'. None of the new people had any connection with the land – but they had accumulated a certain amount of money and so were able to fashion the village to conform to their image of what an idyllic rural community should look like. Shilton began to assume the appearance not of a working agricultural village, but of everyone's idea of a quaint English community.

For many new residents Shilton became a retreat from the harsh realities of twentieth-century urban Britain – literally so in the case of those weekenders who bought property. Shilton offered a tantalizing glimpse of contented village life, far from the daily struggle to survive in the inner city. Shilton provided a chance to escape – at a price. Property values began to rise steeply, narrowing the social status of the people who could afford to move in. So Shilton, in turn, became more and more insulated by its own property values. To live in Shilton is now a sign of considerable social

THE VILLAGE PUB IN SHILTON TODAY

SHILTON
AS IT WAS. . .

attainment. Ironically, once Shilton had been utterly transformed as a community, so it became designated as a conservation area. Local planning policy has ensured that the rural fantasy which Shilton presents to the outside world will now be frozen in aspic.

Socially Shilton has become an exclusive place in which to live. There are few first-time buyers here – and therefore few young children. The village school closed over ten years ago. The shops have gone, too. The post office closed at the end of 1986. The elderly residents of the village now have to find a way to reach Burford or Witney to get their pensions and do their shopping. There is, of course, no public transport. The pub remains open, but few of the new breed of villagers drink there. It relies on the trade from surrounding RAF bases, and from those driving out from nearby towns for a drink in a 'real country pub'. There is no cricket and no football. The church remains and, along with the pub, offers a residual focus for social events. The chapel now struggles to keep going. Shilton residents, however, resist new housing or small business units on the grounds that it would 'spoil' the village.

And so, in some ways, it would. Shilton offers packaged rural life for the well-heeled and the middle aged. Anything new in Shilton, unless, like many of the conversions, it was carefully contrived to look old, would be an intrusion. The package is an attractive one. Visually Shilton is enchanting – self-consciously so. It would be easy to see Shilton as a sanitized version of olde worlde Englande completely divorced from the reality of rural life. But, somewhat worryingly, this is the reality of rural life for very many villages in rural Britain today.

. . .AND AS IT IS TODAY

MILLIE HUNT IS ONE OF THE FEW
REMAINING RESIDENTS OF SHILTON
WHO WERE BORN AND BROUGHT UP
IN THE VILLAGE. SHE STILL RETAINS
THE TRADITION OF THE ENGLISH
COTTAGE GARDEN

─────── ALLENHEADS ───────

Allenheads, as the name implies, lies at the head of Allendale at a point in Northumberland close to the boundary with Cumbria and County Durham. It perches up in the High Pennines and at 1350 feet above sea level Allenheads claims to be England's highest village. Up here on the roof of England farming has always been a struggle against the elements and the many derelict buildings and broken-down stone walls in the area attest to the harshness of the economic as well as the meteorological conditions. Allenheads was never, an agricultural village, even though it was, and is, an estate village. The basis of the economy in Allenheads was mining.

Well into the nineteenth century Allenheads was a thriving community. Hundreds of miners worked locally, taking out lead and fluorspar from beneath the barren hills. During the twentieth century the mine could not compete with overseas imports. Mining began to decline and the population declined with it. During the 1960s the mine closed, then was re-opened and subsequently was closed again. The population dwindled as people moved away in search of employment. Unlike Shilton, Allenheads did not attract newcomers from surrounding towns and cities. It was too remote from large centres of population, isolated by poor roads which in winter could easily be blocked. Although the valley is attractive, it can be bleak. It rains a lot here. The wind blows. An affluent urban middle-class, thinner on the ground in the north-east of England, would not look first at Allenheads for its rustic retreat. So Allenheads became what Shilton would have become without its newcomers – a village in decline. In just a few decades the population plummeted from 750 to 250.

Sporadic attempts by the local estate did little to arrest the decline. The local alternatives to mining – principally forestry and agriculture – were also shedding labour. Allenheads became an ageing village. The younger inhabitants moved to Teeside and further afield for jobs: Allenheads was too remote to make daily commuting possible, especially during the winter. The village was left with an increasingly elderly population, very little in the way of amenities and virtually no economic base. It entered into a vicious spiral of decline and demoralization.

The problems of Allenheads are not those of Shilton. Although both villages, in their way, suffer from social and economic imbalance they result from very different causes. Shilton's problems – in so far as its residents would see themselves as having any – are not those of economic decline, but overheated growth. But Allenheads is a reminder of what our villages would be like if the newcomers had not arrived. Any

village which loses its economic base will decay and die unless someone or something can be found to replace it. In Shilton barns are converted into six-figure weekend residences; in Allenheads barns lie gaunt and derelict along the valley. Shilton may, in the view of some, no longer correspond to an authentic rural community, but the people of Allenheads find authenticity no substitute for their disappearing social fabric. They are much too busy trying to maintain the integrity of the community to worry about such abstract notions.

In 1985 the decline of Allenheads culminated in the closure of the village post office and – the most painful blow of all – the closure of the village inn. A national newspaper published a feature on Allenheads as a dying village. Allenheads began to gather notoriety as a place with no future. But the publicity had a convulsive effect. A village meeting was held in November 1985 in order to reply to the adverse publicity. The community's pride was stung. A committee was elected to try to find ways of overcoming the problems which had afflicted Allenheads. With the help of Northumberland Rural Community Council it organized an appraisal in which questionnaires were distributed around the village, asking the inhabitants to voice their opinions on what was wrong with Allenheads and what was necessary to put it right. The replies focused on unemployment, physical dereliction, the lack of local jobs and the need to find alternative uses for empty and dilapidated buildings. With the assistance of a number of public agencies, a feasibility study was carried out to assess local economic potential. The report recommended the development of a heritage centre in the village, based on its mining history, which would attract tourism. Redundant mine buildings could be brought back into use as small business units. By 1987 work was shortly to get under way. Already the village had been cleaned up and the inn re-opened. There were even plans to build some old peoples' bungalows – the first new houses to be built in Allenheads for 150 years. Thanks to the tenacity of its inhabitants, Allenheads was beginning to fight back.

ACHIEVING A BALANCED COMMUNITY

Self-help and local initiative are giving Allenheads hope for the future. Here there is a recognition that a village must be allowed to develop or it will die. The people of Allenheads have a clear sense of their own priorities. Without a sound economic base their village will simply cease to exist. Everything else about the village must be subordinated to that goal. Shilton, too, possesses a clear view of what it wants. But it

ALLENHEADS WAS A DYING VILLAGE. . .

is a village which can afford to be concerned more about intangible factors – the aesthetics of the village, the view from the drawing-room window. In Shilton development is seen as involving a reduction in the quality of life; in Allenheads without development there will be no life.

Shilton and Allenheads are but two examples of the diversity of villages up and down the countryside of Britain. Their needs are very different and they require resources and policies of an equally different kind to deal with their respective problems. Yet our planning policies towards rural communities do not work like this. Here the commitment to 'every acre counts' is, if anything, even stronger than it is within agricultural policy. Indeed, in recent years the desire to protect the countryside from development has become even more pronounced due to the growth of the environmental movement. Notwithstanding that up to 10 million acres may be in the process of being released from agriculture, we still see rural development as a threat to an exceedingly precious resource.

This suggests that planning policy, as well as agricultural policy, may be overdue for overhaul. We remain saddled with two sets of policies based on the thinking of the 1940s. During the period of post-war reconstruction it was assumed that the rural community could be sustained by a combination of guaranteed agricultural prosperity and a commitment to contain the spread of urban sprawl. The efforts put into preventing the British countryside from disappearing beneath concrete and tarmac have, despite widespread belief to the contrary, been successful. The rate of loss of farmland has been halved since before the war. Thus the rather negative and defensive approach to rural planning has, to a large extent, been able to resist the pressures for wholesale residential and industrial development. But this has arguably been achieved at the cost of distorting the social and economic fabric of the countryside.

In the idealistic days of the 1940s rural planning contained a strong element of progressive social engineering. After three-quarters of a century of almost uninterrupted agricultural depression and relative impoverishment, living standards in rural areas were to be brought up to those of the towns, while at the same time a commitment was made to sustain 'balanced communities' – that is, communities with a mix of different social groups. Paradoxically, rural planning policy, far from being progressive, has systematically had the opposite effect: it has been the most privileged members of rural society who have benefited most, while the poor and deprived have gained comparatively little. On this, at least, Shilton and Allenheads share something in common.

IN VILLAGES WHICH HAVE SUFFERED A LOSS OF THE AGRICULTURAL
POPULATION SIGHTS LIKE THIS WILL BECOME MORE AND
MORE FREQUENT. PATELEY BRIDGE, NORTH YORKSHIRE

The reasons for this state of affairs are by now deeply embedded within the practice of rural planning. For example, planning policies have devoted considerable attention to land use, but rather less to the social needs of the rural population. As a result it has been customary to accept that the 'traditional rural way of life' could be defended by preventing urban encroachment and providing a modicum of basic public services. Translated into planning practice this meant preserving the countryside, almost exclusively, for agriculture. Yet this has occurred precisely at a time when the farming industry has been shedding labour at a historically unprecedented rate. By directing new industrial development away from rural areas conventional planning policy restricted the economic growth of rural Britain and perpetuated a low-wage rural economy for the reduced number of workers who were employed there.

A parallel sequence of events occurred in housing development. New housing was to be restricted – in both the public and the private spheres – so that a planned scarcity of rural housing has duly emerged. Today, not only is public housing in rural areas in chronic short supply, but so is cheap private housing. In the case of both development control policy and housing policy, attempts to preserve the countryside unchanged have backfired – and in a socially regressive manner. Not only does Shilton exemplify this, but even more extreme examples could be drawn from areas like the Lake District where complete villages have been turned into weekend retreats for peripatetic Mancunians, leaving the local working population bereft of any kind of housing within reach of their limited income. Many rural villages, rather than becoming balanced communities with a diverse social mix, have relentlessly become more and more socially exclusive.

By the 1970s there were many in the planning profession who recognized these shortcomings and who were prepared to argue for a more positive conception of rural planning. But by now it was too late. A newly-arrived rural population had its own interests to pursue and having sought its idyllic haven was disinclined to favour intrusive housing and industrial development on its doorstep. A whole new balance of political forces now underlay rural planning policy and its implementation. To the new villagers, more local jobs and more local housing detracted from, rather than enhanced, the quality of rural life. Well-informed and articulate, they soon made their presence felt in the arenas of local decision-making. While sometimes supportive of community development in the abstract, when faced with the prospect of an advance factory or council house development just over *their* fence, they usually objected – and were usually successful.

Such attitudes are particularly prevalent in the south of England and are one factor responsible for environmental protection as a popular rallying cry in recent years. They also explain the continuing popularity of the concept of Green Belts – areas of countryside around major cities from which almost all kinds of development are to be banned. Green Belts have become almost sacrosanct, one of the great political untouchables of 1980s Britain. Although the areas of land formally designated as Green Belt are quite modest, virtually the whole of rural southern England is treated *as if* it were a Green Belt for local political purposes, with numerous counties supporting no-growth or low-growth rural planning policies. Politically ascendent, affluent residents fuel the almost hysterical response to even modest and sensible proposals to adjust planning policies to take account of changing conditions. There is virtually no village which could not support some sensitively designed low-cost housing or small business units, constructed to redress the social imbalance. (See Chapter 7 for examples of what can be achieved.) To do nothing is, in effect, to make things worse.

All the local political pressure in the countryside is, then, towards even tighter control over development and in favour of further protectionism. Yet in the changed conditions of the 1980s it can be argued that we actually need less development control rather than more. This is not to advocate the despoliation of the British countryside, but rather to urge a more balanced approach to positive rural planning. Where *more* planning is needed is not at the local, village level but nationally. We desperately need a national strategy for our countryside which will lay down the balance to be achieved between agriculture and other land uses, and so give guidance to local authorities when local plans are considered. Perversely, current practice is running in the opposite direction: local vetoes over development and no strategic planning to act as a counterbalance. If ever the countryside required strategic thinking it is now. Otherwise Allenheads, if it is successful in finding its feet, will merely become like Shilton. Is that the kind of rural community we want?

PLEASING PROSPECTS

W~HEN WE LOOK AT THE~ countryside – whether spectacular scenery or the more mundane view of field and farm – we all recognize that we are looking at part of our natural heritage. Our landscape is part of our history and our culture: the countryside is part of what it means to be British. It is little wonder, then, that threats to the landscape arouse strong emotions and that the concern to protect the rural environment has become so widespread in recent years.

But if the landscape of Britain is part of our history and culture, the same point can be made in reverse: how we see the countryside is deeply affected by hundreds of years of history and by a culture of western civilization which stretches back over 2000 years. For embedded deep within our culture there lies a strong tradition of pastoral art and poetry which has influenced how we interpret the rural world. Before the late eighteenth century, for example, the Lake District was regarded as a barren area hardly worth visiting. Then, under the influence of the Romantic movement, it came to be accepted as one of Britain's most beautiful regions. Notions of landscape beauty can, and often do, change when viewed in historical perspective.

Today, following the sweeping agricultural changes described in Chapter 2, public appreciation of the rural landscape, and the potential threats to its existence, has never been greater. It is less often appreciated, however, that the beauty of the British landscape owes little to its natural qualities in the strict sense of that term. Hardly any part of the British countryside is a natural wilderness. However remote it may be it is always managed through one form or another of human intervention. The mountains of the Scottish Highlands are, from this standpoint, no less of a managed landscape than the intensively farmed fields of East Anglia. How the landscape looks depends

upon what we, as managers of that environment, do to it. As a nation we end up with the landscape we deserve.

—— LANDSCAPE WITH FIGURES ——

Present opinions about the beauty of the rural landscape are rooted in our past. Take the word 'landscape' itself. Originally it was used to describe a picturesque representation of the countryside – not the land itself, but a painting of it. It was a concept we took from the Dutch who, in the sixteenth century, developed their school of landscape painting. Later the word came to mean a piece of countryside considered as a visual entity, as if it were a picture. This is the literal meaning of the word 'picturesque'. A landscape was thenceforward considered beautiful if it corresponded to the formal compositional rules of a picture. Then, by the eighteenth century, landscape came to refer to the land itself, not to a picture of the land. What began as a term applied to a painting became something which was applied to real terrain. A cultivated pastime developed among the landed aristocracy and gentry to indulge in the contemplation of 'pleasing prospects' – that is, views across a stretch of land which conformed to the compositional rules derived from painting. Such views were eagerly sought and admired by those with a cultivated taste for civilized leisure.

Thus to become a 'pleasing prospect' the real world of the countryside had to correspond to the imaginary world which the landscape painter depicted on his canvas. Where the countryside failed to conform, then it was necessary to rearrange it. The eighteenth-century landowner, anxious to display his aesthetic sensibilities, simply hired an obliging landscape architect or landscape gardener to bring about the transformation. In this way what we have come to accept as picturesque natural beauty was invented and contrived in a way which was certainly like a picture, but rarely natural. Indeed, nature was rearranged to comply with pictorial design and this artefact has henceforth provided a standard by which all landscapes have been judged.

The eighteenth century began the process whereby our ideas of natural beauty became separated from our ideas about a functioning countryside. A working countryside had a picturesque order imposed upon it. Fields were cleared, hedgerows removed, lakes were excavated and hills constructed. Even complete villages were removed and erected elsewhere (one of the best examples is Milton Abbas in Dorset) to provide the landowner with a pleasing prospect from his window or terrace. Arcadia was manufactured. The land itself became the canvas on which to compose a beautiful picture.

Even a wild, open landscape like this is a managed landscape.
Without the sheep to graze these high hills the landscape
would revert to disfiguring scrub

Significantly, agriculture became an *intrusion* into this picturesque vision. The estate owner therefore banished it beyond the park boundary or hid it away behind newly planted belts of trees or artificially constructed mounds. What remained in view was not a working countryside at all but something which was often a work of art to rival those landscapes executed on canvas. A new art form emerged and leading exponents like William Kent, Lancelot (Capability) Brown and Humphry Repton set about changing actual landscapes into pictures. The mundane business of making money should not be allowed to interfere with the civilized contemplation of natural beauty. The practical aspects of agricultural production were therefore banished, literally, out of sight. In every case the criteria which were to be applied to the creation of a pleasing prospect were aesthetic rather than functional.

Landscapes which came to be regarded as the epitome of natural beauty were therefore the antithesis of works of nature. Moreover, farming was only readmitted into this attractive scene if it conformed to accepted aesthetic preferences. Individual pieces of agricultural landscape furniture were allowed, either to enliven the view (animals) or to add a vertical dimension to otherwise undiluted horizontal contours (like picturesque smoke rising from a labourer's cottage). Very occasionally a complete farm might be allowed, not as a subject of profit, but as a rustic embellishment. Those who actually worked on the land became mere figures in a landscape, valuable not so much for what they did, but for how they appeared.

In this way a decisive break occurred between what we have come to regard as natural beauty on the one hand and agricultural necessity on the other. Our appreciation of the countryside has become dominated by this separation between a picturesque and a functional view of the land. Today, almost by definition, what we regard as beautiful tends to be agriculturally unprofitable, while land of high agricultural value is not, on the whole, viewed as picturesque. It then comes as something of a jolt to be confronted by the judgements of those who actually work on the land. Farmers and farm workers, for example, regard a clean, weed-free field as an object of consummate beauty, while wild flowers are weeds which spoil the appearance of the crop. They are impatient with the 'disfiguring' clutter of useless hedgerows and bushes and appreciate the sleek and hygienic design of modern farm buildings. Their view of the landscape is a functional one and almost totally at variance with the prevailing, decidedly non-functional view. It is important to remember when discussing the impact of modern farming methods on the rural landscape that those engaged in agriculture see the land through completely different eyes to the urban dweller. Similarly, prevailing ideas of landscape beauty often

THE CLASSIC UPLAND LANDSCAPE: TROUTBECK, CUMBRIA.
THE HUMANIZED 'IN-BYE' IN THE VALLEY FLOOR CONTRASTS SHARPLY
WITH THE SEMI-NATURAL VEGETATION OF THE OPEN FELLSIDE

MUCH OF THE BEAUTY OF OUR TRADITIONAL LANDSCAPES
DERIVES FROM HUMAN INTERFERENCE. TRADITIONAL
STONE-WALL BOUNDARIES IN NIDDERDALE, YORKSHIRE

ARDINGTON, VILLAGE

THE SOMERSET LEVELS

are an obstacle to understanding the realities of agriculture upon which the landscape is ultimately based.

In recent years these matters have come to a head in the prolonged conflict between farmers and environmentalists over the effects of modern farming methods on what is alleged to be the traditional British landscape. It illustrates vividly how our ideas of landscape beauty have diverged from the economics of contemporary agriculture. This, though, is quite a recent development. Traditionally it has been taken for granted that the major threat to the rural landscape would come from urban development. The countryside simply needed protection from being built upon. Meanwhile the custodianship of the countryside could safely be left in the hands of farmers and landowners. So landscape conservation meant, in effect, keeping urban influences at bay and allowing the stewardship of the farming industry to take its course.

—— DESIGNATED LANDSCAPES ——

Towards the end of the nineteenth century educated opinion began to move in favour of protecting the best British landscapes from the ravages of the Industrial Revolution and the associated spread of cities. The first expression of this was a unique combination of private and public enterprise which has grown to become the largest conservation body in Britain today: the National Trust. The Trust has always operated through the market, ensuring that the majority of its land and buildings are protected through outright purchase. Although the Trust is a private body (and not, as is sometimes supposed, a government organization), it has a unique privilege in English and Scottish law. Its land is 'inalienable' – that is, it cannot be sold. The Trust holds the land in perpetuity, not in order to make a profit (though it must, of course, cover its costs), but in order to preserve it.

Today the Trust owns hundreds of properties and has millions of individual members. It is responsible for many of Britain's most famous stately homes and public gardens. But more importantly from a landscape point of view it owns large stretches of coastline, many commons and open spaces and broad swathes of farmed countryside and woodland. Typically these are located in the most beautiful parts of Britain. The National Trust is a significant presence in the Lake District, for example, where it conducted its first purchase and which remains, in many ways, the Trust's heartland. The Trust does not, though, enjoy any powers of compulsory purchase nor have any particularly privileged place over dealings within the market. Many

more properties are offered to it than it has the resources to acquire and maintain. Although the Trust controls over half a million acres, this represents less than 1 per cent of the British countryside.

Between the wars there was a growing recognition that a voluntary body like the Trust could not hope to guarantee the protection of the countryside on its own. Preservation-by-purchase, while effective, is a painfully slow and expensive process, much dependent upon the right land coming on to the market at the right time. Thus the Trust was in no position to extend the cause of landscape conservation in any significant way when, between 1918 and 1923, over one-quarter of the land in Britain changed hands – the frantic period of land sales which marked the breaking up of many landed estates. Moreover, suburban growth, especially around London, was pushing ever onwards and outwards during this period. There were increasing calls for some form of public intervention in the free-for-all of urban growth and development.

As a result the Council for the Preservation of Rural England (CPRE) was founded in 1926, with similar organizations for Scotland and Wales following in 1927 and 1928. Its first secretary and guiding light was Patrick Abercrombie. The CPRE campaigned for restrictions on urban growth and the removal of unsightly features of contemporary urban life – advertising hoardings, electricity pylons, telegraph poles, mineral workings, etc. – from the countryside. Some limited success was achieved during the 1930s, most notably the restriction of 'ribbon development' out along main roads from urban centres. On the whole, however, attempts to restrict urban sprawl by some form of compulsory planning were piecemeal and largely ineffective. Nevertheless the CPRE and the National Trust were beginning to exert an influence over public opinion which was to achieve its pinnacle in the period immediately following the Second World War.

Throughout the 1930s the CPRE campaigned vigorously for planning legislation which would protect the whole countryside. It also wanted a special status to be granted to the wildest and most beautiful stretches of the countryside, which would be designated as 'National Parks'. These areas would be subject to special protective measures, but equally would be opened up for wider public access (see Chapter 6). Unlike the American National Parks, on which the idea was modelled, these areas would, however, continue to be farmed. Indeed the land would remain in private ownership. The idea achieved fruition in 1949. By Act of Parliament National Parks were established in England and Wales (the system was not extended to Scotland and Northern Ireland) and their organization largely followed the recommendations of

OFTEN THE MOST PAINFUL LOSS IS NOT THE SPECTACULAR
EXAMPLE OF MAGNIFICENT SCENERY, BUT THE LOCAL
LANDSCAPE, WHICH IS MORE INTIMATE AND MORE FAMILIAR

the Dower Report of 1945. Dower initially defined a National Park as:

> . . . an extensive area of beautiful and relatively wild country in which, for the nation's benefit and by appropriate national decisions and action,
> a) the characteristic landscape beauty is strictly preserved,
> b) access and facilities for public open-air enjoyment are amply provided,
> c) wildlife and buildings and places of architectural and historic interest are suitably protected, while
> d) established farming use is effectively maintained.

These objectives remain, but the task of achieving all of them simultaneously has proved to be extremely difficult. There has been ample evidence that some of these objectives are, potentially at least, in conflict with one another. Since 1949 ten National Parks have been designated:

Northumberland – Lake District – Yorkshire Dales – North York Moors – Peak District – Snowdonia – Pembrokeshire Coast – Brecon Beacons – Exmoor – Dartmoor

From time to time the Norfolk Broads has also been recommended for designation, while a proposal in the 1970s to create a Cambrian National Park in mid Wales was defeated by farming interests. The existing National Parks account for less than 10 per cent of England and Wales and although planning restrictions can be draconian they have also been somewhat haphazardly applied. Indeed there is much less unity about the parks than might be supposed. Quite apart from the inevitable variations in local land use, economy and so on, each National Park Authority has placed a different emphasis on the objectives listed above when it has come to planning its future. Originally a National Parks Commission co-ordinated the efforts of the Park Authorities, but in 1968 this was re-named the Countryside Commission and given more general responsibilities for promoting conservation and recreation in the countryside.

The same act which enabled the creation of National Parks also envisaged a 'second division' of protected landscapes which, for one reason or another, could not be absorbed into the parks themselves. These became known as Areas of Outstanding Natural Beauty (AONBs). Unlike the parks there was no specific provision for the encouragement of public recreation and access. Instead AONB designation was solely based on aesthetic criteria and the aim was to preserve the landscape. Today AONBs include stretches of countryside which are less 'wild' than many of the National Parks, but none the less regarded as being among our best-loved landscapes – for example, the Cotswolds, Dedham Vale, the Downs, the Quantock and Mendip Hills, and the Lincolnshire Wolds. Here, too, restrictions on development are extremely tight. In

THE SYSTEM OF LANDSCAPE DESIGNATION HAS HAD TO BE STRICT ENOUGH
TO PRESERVE OUR MOST CHERISHED LANDSCAPE FEATURES WHILE BEING
FLEXIBLE ENOUGH TO ALLOW FARMING TO CONTINUE IN A MODERN,
EFFICIENT FORM, NEAR CARMARTHEN, LLANELLI.

both cases the policy of protection-by-designation has essentially been a negative one: to protect our most important landscapes from the threat of development.

It seems curious that neither Scotland nor Northern Ireland were deemed to possess landscapes worth preserving in this way. It is arguable, of course, that development pressures in these two areas did not warrant it. More likely, however, the explanation is to be found in the differing strength of the farming and landowning interests who have, even in England and Wales, resented the external 'interference' which such designation has appeared to offer. The power to designate National Parks in Northern Ireland was only granted in 1985, while Scotland remains with neither National Parks nor AONBs but 'National Scenic Areas' and regional parks. National Scenic Areas are essentially a planning device whereby local proposals may be referred to the Countryside Commission for Scotland, while attempts to establish regional parks have met severe opposition from the farming lobby.

How important is designation anyway? None of the existing National Parks or AONBs have been preserved in the strict sense of the term. There is a long history of set-piece conflicts over proposals to develop within National Park boundaries, especially mineral workings and trunk roads. Nevertheless in terms of the original debate of the 1930s designation has been reasonably successful: urban development pressures have been held at bay. Unfortunately a new set of problems has arisen to replace the old. The social and economic fabric of many communities in the National Parks has been subject to the changes outlined in the last chapter. Inhibitions on the growth of local sources of employment have exaggerated the changing social balance. Residence 'inside the park' has become an estate agent's cachet. House prices and the status of local inhabitants have risen accordingly.

But perhaps the biggest problem of all has come from an unexpected quarter. Within the National Parks and AONBs, Park Authorities and local councils have exercised powers over land *use*, but they could not control land *management*. The revolution in agriculture not only came upon them unawares, but they found themselves powerless to intervene. For agriculture has been largely exempt from planning control. Yet it has been the management of farmland which has wrought the greatest change on the landscape, one which the system of protection-by-designation was ill-suited to deal with. How ironic that a system which was designed to protect the landscape *for* agriculture should have been undermined by the farming industry itself. Today, the question which has to be asked is, are these landscapes too important to be left in the hands of the farmers themselves?

── LANDSCAPES WITH TEARS ──

The point at which the public perception of farmers changed from being protectors of the rural landscape to its main enemy can be timed quite precisely. It was in 1973 that Sir Colin Buchanan, hitherto a stout defender of our urban heritage from the depredations of the motorway planners, accused farmers, in a speech to the CPRE, of being 'the most ruthless section of the business community'. As he put it, 'The planners and the road engineers have had a good bashing, but they have learnt their lesson. The real danger to the countryside now lies in the agricultural community.'

During the 1970s the protection of the environment became a national political issue. Simultaneously public concern grew over the visible effects of modern farming practice on the rural landscape. As we saw in Chapter 2, the post-war revolution in agricultural technology changed many of the husbandry practices on the farm. These in turn changed the appearance of the countryside – and in ways which, to put it mildly, did not meet with universal approval. Wherever there have been great changes in agricultural technology, the landscape has reflected them. Therefore it is not surprising that it is the landscape of the lowlands – especially the intensive cereals-growing areas like East Anglia – which have changed the most, for it is here that farming has been subject to the most thoroughgoing change.

The greatest controversy has surrounded the disappearance of hedgerows. The countryside, especially the English countryside, owes much of its charm to the characteristic pattern of hedges and trees which not only provide it with a sense of intimacy and scale, but which are an important habitat for many species of plants and animals. There are few places in the world where such a landscape exists, while in Britain many hedgerows are of historic as well as environmental significance, sometimes marking the boundaries of estate and parish. Conventionally the size of fields enclosed by hedges was related to the amount which could be ploughed by a ploughing team in a day. But mechanization has rendered such accounting redundant. Large pieces of machinery need large fields to operate in. A modern combine harvester cannot turn on a sixpence, nor go grubbing about in the crannies and corners at the intersection of hedgerows. Hedges have other disadvantages for the farmer. They are expensive to maintain in an era when labour is not cheap; they take up valuable land which might otherwise be used for a return; and they are no longer needed to restrain stock now that most cereals farmers no longer run sheep or cattle outdoors.

So hedgerows have come out – thousands of miles of them, at the rate of around

4500 miles per year. For the modern cereals farm the ideal environment is the prairie. In Norfolk, for example, 45 per cent of the county's hedgerows were removed between 1946 and 1970 – or 8500 miles. But even those that remain have suffered. Some have been bushwhacked into near-oblivion by machines; others are 'gappy', perfunctory remains of once profuse features. If hedges were to continue to be removed at the same rate as over the last thirty years then by the year 2000 much of the enclosed landscape of the lowlands would cease to exist.

The removal of hedgerows has often been the most obvious sign of agricultural change. However, other important landscape features have also been removed, threatening to reduce the lowland countryside to featureless prairie. Traditional, broadleaf woodlands have disappeared in large numbers, many bulldozed away to make room for more acreage under the plough, others being felled and replanted with more profitable, but alien, conifers. Other landscape features have also been affected. Ponds have been filled, wetlands drained, heaths have been ploughed up and hay meadows ploughed and re-seeded. It has all added up to a loss of diversity in the lowland landscape, a tendency to reduce the countryside to an ordered, and bland, uniformity lacking the local distinctiveness and sheer haphazardness which gives our countryside its elements of delight and serendipity. Instead large tracts of lowland countryside now possess the rational geometry of the accountant's spreadsheet.

BLENDING IN MODERN AGRICULTURE WITH TRADITIONAL LANDSCAPES
IS SOMETIMES A DIFFICULT EXERCISE: NEAR LULWORTH, DORSET

Landscape change in the uplands has been less severe, but upland landscapes remain vulnerable none the less. The classic uplands landscape results from the juxtaposition of bare open fells, moor and mountain with the humanized 'in-bye' of the valley floor with its fields and human artefacts, together with dense woodland on the steep valley sides. The major change is that the semi-natural vegetation used for rough grazing on the hills is disappearing at an increasing rate. In many cases it is being 'improved' – that is ploughed up and re-seeded for intensive grassland cultivation. Elsewhere it has been replaced by forestry – and the insensitive design (or non-design) of many coniferous forests has attracted widespread criticism. The 'serried ranks' of conifers stretching across the hills have become notorious for their effect on the landscape of the uplands. In recent years the Forestry Commission has become more aware of its responsibilities to the landscape, but whenever trees are more profitable than sheep or cattle and softwoods are more profitable than hardwoods then the trend towards more conifer-covered hills will continue.

The uplands, too, have been affected by changes in field boundaries. Stone walls and hedge banks have been removed (often to be replaced by wire fencing) or been neglected. The character of the upland landscape is, indeed, affected by the delicate balance between agricultural prosperity and decline. Traditionally the greatest threats to the landscape have emerged from the problems of poverty, neglect and decay. The results may sometimes look picturesque – as in the case of antiquated farm buildings – but broken walls, derelict farmsteads and scrub-covered hillsides often present disfiguring eyesores. Equally the zeal for 'improvement' during periods of agricultural prosperity can wreak changes on a par with the lowlands. Heather moorland may disappear under the plough; new farm buildings of a scale and design out of keeping with their surroundings bespatter the countryside; and 'arablization' invades the valley floor. For all their robust resistance to the elements, upland landscapes are often the result of a fragile balance which requires subtle management.

In many areas the scale and the pace of landscape change has caused considerable resentment, whether from the village newcomer or the urban visitor. Many farmers have responded to this hostility with a mixture of anger and disdain. The anger has arisen because many farmers believe that allegations that they are 'ruining' the countryside are exaggerated and too indiscriminate. They complain about conservationists' widespread ignorance of the economics of modern food production. Farmers are quick to point out that the desire to retain hedgerows and other familiar landscape features emanates from exactly that social group – the 'urban mass' – whose demands

for cheap food have indirectly brought about the changes which they so deplore. The farmer therefore accuses the environmental lobby of hypocrisy. This charge is often returned by environmentalists who note how much farmers claim the 'stewardship' of the countryside on behalf of the nation while demanding an exclusive right to decide upon how it should be managed. Needless to say, once the battle lines have been drawn in this way, there tends to be a deterioration in relationships all round.

Those organizations, most notably the Countryside Commission, which have attempted to reconcile these viewpoints have faced a difficult task. Established stereotypes tend to lead to self-fulfilling behaviour. Farmers, their pride stung, can easily become aggressively unhelpful to even the most politely-expressed and well-reasoned appeal to curb some of the unnecessarily destructive aspects of their farming activity. Equally there are farmers who feel a sense of guilt at taking out a hedge or destroying a copse of trees for purely economic reasons and farmers, no less than anyone else, do not like to be reminded of something which, in the abstract, they might find difficult to justify. Touched on a raw nerve, they can react accordingly.

The belief that much environmental conflict is due to a 'breakdown of communications' has been behind a number of attempts to reconcile farming practice with the conservation of the countryside. The Countryside Commission has conducted projects on 'demonstration farms' to show how profitable agriculture may be accompanied by conservation management. The current chairman of the Countryside Commission, Sir Derek Barber, has also been a driving force behind the establishment at a county level of Farming and Wildlife Advisory Groups (FWAGs) which, from the late 1970s onwards, have attempted to put voluntary conservation into practice. The Commission has also grant-aided numerous individual projects on farms (especially tree planting) and has made a valuable contribution to preserving many landscape features through its numerous countryside management schemes. But faced with a tidal wave of agricultural change the Countryside Commission has, at best, only been able to offer a minor palliative. Even the Commission's own evaluations of landscape change have not claimed more than limited, and often fragile, success.

For although communication and education have, from time to time, been a problem, they have not been the whole problem. A direct conflict of interest has also been involved. Farmers regard the landscape as a factor of production and a source of profit; supporters of the environmental movement, on the other hand, look upon the countryside as a source of visual pleasure, of recreation and of enjoyment – as something to be 'consumed'. While the public's idea of a 'pleasing prospect' tends to

be so divorced from a farmer's idea of the profitable use of his land, then this conflict will remain. Attempts at persuasion have frequently achieved little more than to give farmers guilty consciences as they proceed to grub out their hedgerows. While the economic incentives have remained, little, it has seemed, short of compulsion will lead to more environmentally desirable landscape change. From the late 1970s onwards the battle has been to find the best mix of compulsion, incentive and education which will integrate agriculture with landscape conservation.

——— THE BATTLE FOR EXMOOR ———

Exmoor is where the modern environmental lobby may be said to have cut its teeth. During the late 1970s a bitter and prolonged dispute took place here over the conversion of moorland to intensive grassland cultivation. Although the dispute was local in character it was recognized by all parties as having national significance, for it was on Exmoor that the feasibility of various landscape conservation options were tested. Was National Park designation an effective means of securing our cherished landscapes? Was it politically feasible to bring agriculture within the planning process? Was the voluntary approach to conservation capable of being made to work, or was a compulsory element unavoidable? The set-piece conflict on Exmoor was to influence the answers to all of these questions.

Owing to its climate and topography Exmoor has long been the most vulnerable of the National Parks to the 'improvement' of its heather moorland. Exmoor farmers, in common with those elsewhere, were encouraged, from the Second World War onwards, to maximize their profits and land values by improving the productivity of their land. An estimated 9500 acres of moorland were reclaimed between 1947 and 1976, out of 59,000 acres within the Exmoor National Park. For many years the Exmoor Society, a vociferous and well-connected preservationist pressure group, had voiced its opposition. It argued that Exmoor was being robbed of precisely that quality which had led to its designation as a National Park in the first place.

In 1968 the National Park Authorities in Exmoor designated 41,000 acres of moorland as a Critical Amenity Area and reached a 'gentleman's agreement' with the National Farmers Union and the Country Landowners Association whereby farmers in the area would voluntarily give six months' notice to the Park Authorities of intention to plough. In return the Park Authorities agreed to desist from invoking a 'Section 14 order' under the 1968 Countryside Act which would make such

THE KIND OF LANDSCAPE CHANGE WHICH PROVOKED THE CONFLICT
ON EXMOOR. THE IMPROVED GRASSLAND IN THE MIDDLE
DISTANCE CONTRASTS MARKEDLY WITH THE UNIMPROVED
HEATHER MOORLAND IN THE FOREGROUND. WITHOUT THE
RESTRICTIONS RECOMMENDED BY THE PORCHESTER REPORT
ALL OF EXMOOR MIGHT HAVE BEEN 'IMPROVED' IN THIS MANNER

notification compulsory. The Park Authorities hoped in this way to persuade farmers to enter into management agreements which would conserve the moorland. Between 1968 and 1977, however, a further 1000 to 1500 acres of moorland were ploughed up, including 650 acres within the Critical Amenity Area between 1972 and 1977, assisted by, among other things, grants from the Ministry of Agriculture.

During 1976 the Exmoor Society became increasingly angry at the continuing loss of moorland and allegations began to fly around in the local and national press that the Exmoor National Park Committee was 'soft on farmers' or had been infiltrated by agricultural interests. It was also noted that although nineteen proposals to plough had been notified between 1969 and 1973 not a single management agreement had been negotiated. The NFU and CLA were not prepared to accept any serious restrictions on farming activity without compensation; and equally the Park Authority was not prepared to pay the level of compensation demanded by farmers. The Countryside Commission, in its role of National Parks overlord, also became concerned. It regarded the case of Exmoor as an opportunity to push for further powers of compulsory purchase of land in the National Parks, and against the opposition of the NFU and CLA proposed that, in effect, the improvement of open moorland and similar 'material changes of use' should be defined as 'development' and become subject to planning permission.

The prospect of internecine warfare between the Department of the Environment and the Ministry of Agriculture was avoided by the appointment of Lord Porchester, a landowner and chairman of Hampshire County Council, to conduct a study of Exmoor with a view to recommending a solution to their predicament. The Porchester report was published in November 1977. It concluded that the voluntary system of notification and management agreements was not working, but it also rejected the Countryside Commission's proposals as too cumbersome. He recommended instead that a new survey should be carried out, aimed at tightening up the existing Critical Amenity Area Map, so that within this area a 'final commitment' could be made to conservation and accordingly a presumption made against agricultural reclamation. The Ministry of Agriculture was also urged to withdraw grant aid for improvement within the area. The Park Authority should be given the power to make Moorland Conservation Orders, binding in perpetuity, in return for which farmers would receive compensation equivalent to the resultant decline in land values.

Most of the recommendations were accepted, but with one very important proviso. At the very last gasp the National Park Committee concluded a management

agreement with the Glenthorne Estate, which occupied the heart of Exmoor, whereby compensation was paid on the basis of the annual profit foregone by agreeing to conserve. This established the principle, for which the NFU and CLA had been campaigning, that compensation could be assessed for a hypothetical loss of profits generated by agricultural subsidies. This seemed an erratic interpretation of the notion of 'stewardship', as well as offering an interesting principle of public compensation for the withdrawal of public support. It was a principle which was to be at the heart of forthcoming legislation embodied in the Wildlife and Countryside Act (see Chapter 5), even though in many cases it would have been cheaper to buy the land outright.

Legislation incorporating the Porchester proposals was lost in the run up to the 1979 General Election. Nevertheless subsequent negotiations produced an agreement which has stuck: since 1978 the reclamation of Exmoor within the critical Amenity Area has been brought to a halt. This is partly because the negotiated 'going rate' for compensation has been generous; and partly because the downturn in the farming economy has made moorland improvement less attractive. The result of the conflict on Exmoor has been a kind of stop-gap compromise. Pragmatically reclamation has been halted and farming activity has thereby been restricted; but farmers have won an important claim to be compensated for their putative 'loss'. The system is, however, a reactive one: to obtain assistance a farmer must first threaten to plough up moorland. Those landowners who have no intention of ploughing up Exmoor, such as the National Trust, cannot be offered financial help to manage their land for conservation. So at the centre of the system there remains a somewhat negative and defensive sanction-by-designation approach.

Today the threats to the landscape of Exmoor come from elsewhere. One is the familiar threat of afforestation. A second is more subtle and not immediately recognizable, for while the battle was being fought over reclamation the husbandry regime on the unreclaimed moorland was changing. EEC policy as it applied to Less Favoured Areas like Exmoor was altering the balance of profitability between sheep and beef cattle production. Farmers were switching into sheep, encouraged to do so by subsidies offered through the European sheepmeat regime. As a result bracken is pushing through the heath all over Exmoor. Sheep which do not eat the young bracken shoots have pushed out the cattle, which did. As a result, in twenty years' time there might no longer be any heather on Exmoor to contribute to its landscape.

All this suggests that a more comprehensive approach to conservation is required for areas like Exmoor. Short-term solutions bolted on to agricultural policy as an

afterthought are unlikely to resolve the conflicts of interest between farmers under pressure to preserve their profitability and conservationists concerned to retain the rural landscape. In order to be effective landscape conservation cannot remain in a position where it constantly runs after agricultural change, breathlessly attempting to catch up with a system over which it has little influence. The lesson from Exmoor is that a set-piece conflict, however necessary to publicize a desperate situation, will not in itself secure a long-term solution. The integration of agriculture and conservation cannot proceed by lurching from one local site to another. Instead agricultural policy must be formulated in such a way that farmers do not need to choose between conservation and profitability.

—— THE ESAs ARE COMING ——

The dispute on Exmoor had repercussions far beyond its boundaries. It was on Exmoor that the conservation movement attempted to hold the line against hitherto relentless agricultural change. It achieved a modest degree of success, not least because it focused the attention of a wider public, through the publicity the dispute received, on the broader issues involved. So Exmoor was a test-bed. The combatants flexed their muscles, with half an eye on government, and agreed, in the end, to a grudgingly acceptable compromise. Exmoor was significant, partly because it placed farmers and landowners on the defensive for the first time, and undermined their public image as custodians of the countryside. From that point on landscape conservation was placed firmly on the political agenda.

As the Exmoor dispute subsided, so the spotlight shifted to hitherto obscure local sites similarly threatened by the onrush of modern agriculture – Amberley Wild Brooks, Gedney Grove End, Halvergate Marshes . . . the roll-call of conflicts between modern farming and environmental conservation. During the 1980s, however, there has been a recognition among conservationists that the rural landscape cannot be safeguarded either by designation or by rushing from one site to another bringing pressure to bear on farmers and landowners. Landscape conservation has meant tackling the root cause of the problem – the nature of the agricultural system which has brought about unwelcome landscape change.

In recent years, conservationists have moved in on debates about the future of agricultural policy. They have joined in the chorus of criticism against food surpluses and the cost of maintaining a hi-tech farming system which is so destructive of the

DECIDUOUS WOODLAND HAS BEEN DISAPPEARING FROM RURAL BRITAIN
AT AN ALARMING RATE. IT IS HOPED THAT THE INTRODUCTION
OF ESAs WILL LEAD TO ITS RETENTION ALONG WITH OTHER IMPORTANT
LANDSCAPE FEATURES. WINDERMERE, CUMBRIA

landscape. They have also seized the political opportunities presented by the prospect of serious structural change in British agriculture (see Chapter 2). If land is now becoming 'surplus' to agricultural requirements, the conservationist lobby argues, then why cannot farming policy be reviewed to take account of this new situation? Perhaps the economic necessity to encourage farmers to intensify their farming methods and engage in further rounds of landscape change no longer exists. Since education and persuasion have achieved little, the argument runs, perhaps now is the time when money can be made to talk. Farm support could be redirected away from encouraging further intensification and towards encouraging the kinds of landscapes that the nation wishes to see retained. If every acre no longer counts for farm production, perhaps some thought could be give to farming for landscape objectives.

Well, the Ministry of Agriculture has not yet become the Department of the Environment, but it has taken some modest steps in that direction. The writing is on the wall for open-ended commitments to ever increasing farm production, and as a result both the ministry and the farming organizations have shown themselves more amenable to the conservationist cause. Here the principle of compensation, conceded on Exmoor, is significant. If farmers can no longer make money from surpluses, perhaps there are possibilities in conservation? In 1987 the ministry announced a scheme which encouraged farmers to adjust some of their practices to help sustain treasured landscapes, wildlife habitats and archaeological sites. It designated six Environmentally Sensitive Areas (ESAs) in England and Wales within which special financial assistance, on a fairly generous level, was to be given to farmers and landowners who voluntarily agreed to promote farming practices which maintained or improved the local environment. Twelve further ESAs were proposed later in the year. Furthermore, the British government was successful in obtaining EEC assistance for this initiative via an amendment to the regulations which form part of the CAP.

The ESAs have followed from another *ad hoc* solution to a set-piece environmental conflict, this time in the Halvergate Marshes of Norfolk. This dispute has a number of parallels with the earlier conflict on Exmoor. In the case of Halvergate – an otherwise unremarkable area of the Norfolk Broads – agricultural improvement and river drainage schemes were threatening to transform unimproved pasture into lucrative cereals land. Until the dispute blew up, few people visited Halvergate and virtually no one lived there, but its importance lay in the fact that it was the last remaining stretch of open grazing marsh in eastern England. When, in late 1980, a proposal was made to drain and improve the land it presented a classic case of all that was unsatisfactory with

public policy over farming and conservation. The conversion of Halvergate would not have been viable without the hefty subsidies on offer from the Ministry of Agriculture. But the farming organizations, as on Exmoor, demanded compensation for not proceeding with a scheme which could never have gone ahead without financial support from the public purse in the first place.

For over three years a cat-and-mouse game was played between the farming and conservation interests, their local representatives and government sponsors. In 1985 an experimental Broads Grazing Marshes Conservation Scheme was introduced aimed at making the local grazing regime as financially attractive as cereals growing. Farmers were paid £123 per hectare (=2.4 acres) if they joined the scheme (90 per cent did so). But on this scale conservation is expensive: £1.7 million for the Halvergate scheme and over £5 million per annum for the 232,000 hectares covered by the first six ESAs.

The ESAs work in a similar way to the Broads experiment. Farmers are offered acreage payments in return for a commitment to manage farmland in ways which maintain – or improve – the special character of the countryside. The payments vary from area to area – indeed, one of the strengths of the scheme is that it is sufficiently flexible to respond to local requirements. By restraining agricultural output ESA schemes are intended to achieve four objectives:

• protection for landscape, wildlife, archaeological and historical features
• income-support for traditionally-run farms which must remain viable if such features are to survive
• a limitation on the conversion of land to production which contributes to surpluses
• the encouragement of less-intensive farming.

The initial list of ESAs is quite diverse: West Penwith in Cornwall, the Cambrian Mountains, the Downs, Swaledale and Dentdale in Yorkshire, the Somerset Levels and the Norfolk Broads. After some initial suspicion of becoming 'glorified park wardens' and of external interference (in what many farmers would probably have done anyway), the rate of participation by farmers has been encouraging. However the ESAs have been embraced only with some reluctance by government: the initial list of sites suggested to the ministry was 140. Of these only six were initially designated, and defined in a very restrictive way. There *are* encouraging aspects to the ESA scheme, provided that it is taken up in a serious way. At present they cost £5 million out of the £2.2 billion expended on the production of surplus food. This suggests, at best, a modest environmental fig-leaf placed over the more unacceptable

parts of conventional farming policy. But at least the precedent has now been established for the redirection of farming support.

The resolution of the many conflicts between farmers and environmentalists over landscape conservation thus remains a very hit-and-miss affair. The trick may be to make the maintenance of attractive landscapes coincide with profitable farming, but this in turn means fashioning an agricultural policy which allows this to happen. It is not clear how far we, the public, are prepared to pay for this, even at the cost of more expensive food. There is, of course, no reason why the conservation of the countryside should be expensive. It has become so because of the way in which the current maelstrom of policies has emerged. This is even more clear when we turn to consider the conservation of wildlife, for clearly changes in the use and management of land have affected not only the rural landscape, but the range of available habitats for our native fauna and flora. And here, over the last decade, the conflict has been prolonged indeed.

LANDSCAPE CHANGE ON EXMOOR.
IN THE FOREGROUND PLOUGHED AND RE-SEEDED GRASSLAND CONTRASTS WITH
THE TRADITIONAL SEMI-NATURAL VEGETATION IN THE DISTANCE

A Natural World

Agriculture, by definition, involves a disturbance of the natural ecology of the countryside. Indeed, most forms of agriculture do not so much disturb the natural environment as destroy it and replace it by a man-made artefact. It is hardly surprising, then, that in the last two decades agriculture has been at the forefront of the debate over man's relationship to the environment.

In the previous chapter we examined the impact of agriculture on the landscape. Ultimately our decision about whether modern farming has either improved or damaged the landscape of rural Britain, can only be a subjective one: it all depends upon what we regard as beautiful. There are many farmers who believe that modern landscapes are an improvement on the past, equally there are many members of the public who do not. But the impact of farming on the ecology of the countryside – on the range and quality of the wildlife which it supports – can be objectively measured. Over the last twenty years evidence has accumulated about the effects of modern farming practice on our natural flora and fauna which has given increasing cause for concern.

To some extent this concern parallels that over the effect on landscapes. Clearly the two are very closely connected. A change in land use or the management of a farm will not only bring about changes in the landscape, but affect the habitats of plants, animals and birds. Looked at visually the countryside is a collection of landscapes, but from an ecological standpoint it is a collection of wildlife habitats. And in the view of many conservationists our wildlife is no less a part of our national heritage than our rural landscapes.

GREEN UNPLEASANT LAND

As we saw in the last chapter, public opinion during the immediate post-war period was happy to leave the custodianship of the countryside in the hands of farmers and landowners. Planning restrictions were introduced to protect the countryside from the towns, but said little about how the countryside itself was to be managed. Agriculture was, for the most part, exempt from planning legislation.

Concern that something might be amiss emerged during the early 1960s. The first signs of public disillusionment with agriculture began with criticisms of its excessive use of chemicals. This was sparked off in 1962 by the publication of a book, *Silent Spring*, by the American scientist Rachel Carson. It was she who first drew attention to the consequences for wildlife of the indiscriminate use of pesticides. With relentless detail she documented the effects of the petrochemical 'elixirs of death'. She did not argue that chemical pesticides should never be used, but she did condemn their thoughtless use by individuals largely ignorant of their consequences. 'Future generations', she wrote, 'are unlikely to condone our lack of prudent concern for the integrity of the natural world that supports all life.'

With words like these Rachel Carson placed farming practice at the centre of what was to be an often bitter controversy about the desire to maintain an efficient, profitable and cheap system of food production with the ecological balance of the countryside. Her argument was not based on idyllic sentiment, but on cool, scientific analysis, which undoubtedly made it all the more effective. She recognized that agriculture was bound to disturb the natural ecology and that ecological change was both inevitable and, properly handled, desirable. But she feared that the countryside being fostered by modern agriculture was neither safe nor sustainable in the long term.

Her attack was not, therefore, directed at the use of chemicals in general, but the indiscriminate adoption of some chemicals in particular. She singled out organo-chloride insecticides – entirely novel synthetic substances which no species, including human beings, had previously encountered. When they were first introduced (during the 1940s) they were an enormous boon to the farmer and the initial response was enthusiastic. The most common, the insecticide DDT, was effective and cheap to manufacture. It was used extensively during the Second World War and is still used in parts of the Third World. DDT was followed by others from the same chemical family – aldrin, isodrin, entrin and dieldrin – which were widely used in Britain as sheep-dips and seed-dressings.

When they were introduced no one knew how these insecticides actually worked. They were, however, very stable and had no discernible effect on humans so it was assumed they were safe. Yet it was this very stability which made them so potentially harmful, for once these artificial substances were released into the environment, they stayed around. This was an attraction to farmers, who did not want the effects to disappear after the next rain shower, but no one thought through what this might mean for the ecosystem as a whole. It was Rachel Carson who first brought to the attention of a wider public just what these unintended consequences might be and the chain reaction which farmers had inadvertently set up.

The best-known example was the accumulation of toxic substances in the food chain. So stable were these chemicals that they were passed on from prey to predator, involving a metabolic process which led to higher and higher concentrations as they were passed along. In Britain Rachel Carson's vision of a 'silent spring' provided a potent symbol of the dangers. Few people cared about the disappearance of possibly harmful insects, but there were few who were not moved by the prospect of losing entire species of birds. Those under threat included some of the most majestic of all birds – golden eagles, peregrine falcons – because, as birds of prey, they were at the head of the food chain. The danger was not so much from direct poisoning, but from the effect of less than lethal doses on eggshell thinning. This produced a spectacular decline in the number of young birds successfully reared – and eventually in the total population of adult birds. For example, in areas where golden eagles fed extensively on carrion sheep which had been dipped in dieldrin, the proportion of pairs successfully rearing young fell from 72 to 29 per cent during the late 1950s. Peregrine falcons were reduced by half in little over two decades. Eventually restrictions were placed on the use of aldrin and dieldrin as seed dressings in 1962 and the use of dieldrin as a sheep dip in 1966. When DDT was found to cause cancer in humans it, too, was restricted. Unfortunately the stability of these compounds, which originally was their attraction, has ensured that the rate of recovery of the affected species has been slow.

Further research by agrochemical manufacturers has enabled these persistent organo-chlorides to be superseded by others more selective and less far-reaching in their effects. Nevertheless the indirect consequences cannot always be foreseen. Resistant strains of pests have developed in response to the introduction of pesticides. This has led, in turn, to the development of new pesticides to kill off the new pests, which have led to new strains of mutants, leading to. . . . And so the spiral continues. Certainly there seems little end to modern agriculture's use of chemicals, nor to the

STUBBLE-BURNING IS AN ACCEPTED PART OF EFFICIENT
MODERN FARMING. IT HAS, HOWEVER, MADE FARMERS LESS THAN
POPULAR WITH THEIR NEIGHBOURS AND DOES LITTLE FOR THE
IMMEDIATE APPEARANCE OF THE LANDSCAPE

discovery of yet another pest which needs another chemical to cope with it. Science fiction fantasies of plagues of mutant pests devastating the countryside can be discounted. But some pesticides have had a boomerang effect by wiping out natural predators or by obligingly clearing the way for another, equally troublesome, pest. This has led to modest attempts to introduce natural forms of pest control rather than rely on further doses of chemicals. Far more likely, however, is a future in which pest control will be handled by biotechnology – genetically engineered substances which will either eliminate pests or allow pest-resistant strains of plants, etc. to be bred. Meanwhile, the temptation to reach for the sprayer is often irresistible.

As farms become more specialized, so they become more vulnerable to infestation. The use of chemicals on farms today is by no means directed solely towards insects. Modern cultivation methods demand a much wider array of chemicals. The least threatening sometimes seems to be fertilizers. Modern high-yielding hybrid varieties of cereals, for example, require large amounts of fertilizer to be successful. But fertilizers make weeds as well as cereals grow. So large doses of fertilizer are accompanied by frequent sprays of herbicides to kill off the weeds. Such weeds are often commonly known as wild flowers. Poppies, for example, are eliminated from modern fields of wheat. They clear the way for wild oats, a much tougher customer which requires the application of an expensive, specialist spray. This reduction of field plant varieties creates the risk of aphid attack, requiring further spraying. It is quite common for tractors to have to trundle up and down a field nine or ten times in a single season. For those who are alarmed by this prospect it is worth pointing out that most suburban lawns receive higher concentrations of chemicals than the typical farmer's field – and for similar reasons: they make cultivation less hard work.

This comparison places the use of agrochemicals in perspective, but the threats to the ecology of the countryside are real enough. Trundling tractors compact the soil; the use of artifical rather than natural fertilizers also affects soil structure. Some of the consequences are less direct and take a longer period to become manifest. In East Anglia nitrogenous fertilizers have seeped into acquifers (underground lakes) – the process can take twenty-five years – and threatened to poison water supplies. Fertilizer which runs off fields into drainage channels and rivers also creates eutrophication – the excessive growth of aquatic plants and the removal of oxygen from the water, which in turn kills the fish. Waste products from livestock farms also threaten to pollute water courses. It seems ironic that the excessive specialization of modern British agriculture has created a situation in which cereals farms apply over 1

million tons of artificial fertilizer each year, while intensive livestock producers have difficulty disposing of their accumulated slurry.

Public unease about the impact of modern farming on the environment grew from the 1960s onwards. It was not limited to the use of chemicals. The destructive impact of agriculture on the range of wildlife habitats which have traditionally formed the mosaic of the British countryside also aroused widespread concern. This was given a sharp focus by the publication in 1980 of Marion Shoard's book, *The Theft of the Countryside*, an impassioned attack upon farmers for bringing about the ruination of the rural environment. As a polemic it was an outstanding success, comparing with *Silent Spring* as a book which decisively influenced public opinion on the conservation of the countryside. It also placed the farming lobby markedly on the defensive. In alarming and relentless detail Marion Shoard charted the ways in which modern agricultural methods were despoiling the countryside. Her arguments struck a national chord; the campaign for a change in the direction of agricultural policy took off.

Shoard's book described the technological transformation and the 'subsidies for destruction' which threatened the future of the countryside. It detailed the impact on seven types of landscape feature, each of which constituted an important wildlife habitat and which together provided the unique diversity of rural Britain.

Hedgerows

Hedgerows are not only important landscape features, but they also shelter significant populations of wildlife. They harbour many of our common mammals – hedgehogs, voles, moles, mice, stoats, weasels and shrews. They feed upon the multitude of slugs, snails, spiders and insects in the tangled undergrowth, while they in turn are preyed upon by owls and kestrels. The hedges themselves, especially the more ancient ones, are a varied assortment of species, some, like honeysuckle, holly, hawthorn and wild rose, attractive in their own right. If hedgerows were to continue to be removed

MARGINAL LAND ON THE SOMERSET LEVELS

at the rate of the last thirty years, it has been calculated that 250 plant species would be severely diminished, and up to thirty could disappear altogether in certain areas.

Hedgerow trees

As hedgerows have come out so too have the trees which have traditionally been planted within them. During the 1970s an estimated 11 million elms were lost due to Dutch Elm Disease, but over twice this number of deciduous species have been deliberately taken out since the war. In the south of Britain these trees have mainly been oak, beech and chestnut; in the north, wych elm, ash and sycamore are more common. The oak alone supports 284 species of insect and is a food plant for 114 species of moth. But trees can be a nuisance for modern farming. They shade the crop, drain the soil of minerals and spread a tangle of roots which interfere with cultivation. So they have come out – and even where hedgerows remain, modern flail-cutters give sapling trees little hope of survival.

Woods

Deciduous woodlands are among the richest of wildlife habitats, but they have been diminished by two processes: complete clearance to make way for more profitable crops; and replanting with conifers, which from an ecological point of view sometimes amounts to the same thing. Although there are large regional variations, up to 30 per cent of broadleaved woodlands have been destroyed in little over twenty years. The result is often a severe loss for wildlife. The oak may support 284 species, but the fir supports only sixteen. The dense, all-year canopy of the conifer wood admits little light. The woodland floor does not support plants like bluebells, primroses or wood anemones; only fungi can flourish. The missing plants are not replaced by others.

Roughlands

Traditional farming methods left plenty of bits and pieces of uncultivated or semi-cultivated land to provide a range of habitats for wildlife. As agriculture has become more rationalized and as the value of land has increased, so these patches of land have either been brought into cultivation or new farming methods have transformed them. They include such diverse habitats as hay meadows, water meadows, chalk downland turf, lowland heaths, moors, cliff-tops and coastal marshland. As we saw in the last chapter the higher slopes of heath, moor and down have been steadily ploughed up and re-seeded with ryegrass. The lower-lying marshes and meadows have been drained and converted to cereals production. Some of these habitats are especially rich. Chalk downland turf in Dorset alone supports 120 species of wild flowers, including seven kinds of orchids. It has been estimated that present trends in the

'improvement' of farmland could eliminate 95 per cent of our butterfly species. Already one, the Large Blue butterfly, has apparently been rendered extinct since 1979.

Downs

Downland turf could once be found across large stretches of southern and eastern England. Now it is largely confined to steep slopes. Chalk downlands are best known for their abundance of wild flowers. But the profitability of cereals since the Second World War has sounded the death knell for large areas of downland. Vast areas of Dorset and Wiltshire, for example, have been turned into a barley prairie, ablaze not with harebells and scabious, but only burning straw and stubble. Less than 3 per cent of the chalk downland of Wessex now remains intact.

Moors

Britain's moorland supports some of our most spectacular birds – especially birds of prey. As we have seen, because they are at the head of the food chain they are uniquely vulnerable, even though nothing (other than man) preys on them. Ploughing up moorland not only affects the landscape; it takes away the habitat for insects, small birds and mammals which form the diet of native birds of prey. Yet moorland has been lost at an increasing rate since the war as the familiar mixture of economic pressure and incentives has led to agricultural improvement and ecological decline.

Wetlands

Any wetland, from a pond to a lake or marsh, usually supports a wide variety of wildlife. But wetlands everywhere have been under threat. Farms without horses do not need ponds, so they have been filled into satisfy the rational symmetry of modern field patterns. Water meadows have been drained and reclaimed either for cereals production or intensive grassland. Since the draining of the Fens in the seventeenth century, potentially fertile marshes have also been turned into productive arable land. Rivers, too, have been dredged and straightened out, turning meandering water courses into geometrically sterile canals. So rich is their wildlife and so diminished are their number, that the preservation of wetlands has been at the centre of recent conflicts between the farming and environmental lobbies. We shall look in detail at one *cause célèbre*, the Somerset Levels, below.

The almost relentless pursuit of agricultural production has thus brought about a measurable decline in environmental diversity. The once commonplace has often become rare, while the once rare has become precious indeed – or even, like the Large Blue butterfly, extinct. Because agriculture lay outside the planning system those

THE MAINTENANCE OF WETLANDS IS OFTEN A MATTER
OF CAREFUL MANAGEMENT. THE NATURE OF THE DRAINING
REGIME IS CRUCIAL. NEITHER TOO LITTLE NOR TOO MUCH
DRAINING IS REQUIRED. SOMERSET LEVELS

individuals or organizations concerned by the direction of agricultural change have been powerless to oppose it. Marion Shoard's achievement was to contribute decisively towards shifting this balance of power. The general public, which throughout the 1970s was becoming increasingly alarmed by what was happening to the countryside, began to realize that a voluntary system of conservation was not enough. Some kind of legislative control was needed.

—— THE SOMERSET LEVELS ——

Towards the end of 1977, while Lord Porchester was deliberating on the future of Exmoor (see Chapter 4) the next set-piece conflict over agriculture and the environment emerged in Somerset. Between the Mendips and the Quantocks there lay the Somerset Levels, 170,000 acres of low-lying marshy meadowland created by the flood plains of eight rivers as they sluggishly meander towards the Bristol Channel. The landscape is not spectacular and the Levels are not within a National Park. But the area possesses an undoubted charm, a more verdant and intimate version of the Fens. It also possesses that unique quality of the British countryside to lose its visitor in an apparently timeless and tranquil oasis, a world removed from the 'zip-strip' of the M5, even though it crosses the western edge of the Levels.

Ecologically the Somerset Levels are unique. Each winter there are floods and for hundreds of years farmers have battled against the level of the rivers. The silt fertilizes the land and has created a rich peaty loam – fence posts hammered into the soil promptly sprout into mature trees. The meadows support lush grazing for dairy cattle, but also a wide variety of wild flowers, some of them rare. The water courses are edged with reeds, sedges, flag irises, water lilies, kingcups and many other marshland plants. There is a profuse presence of amphibious life – frogs, toads, newts – and mammals such as voles, mice, shrews and – rarest of all – otters. The Levels are internationally renowned for their birdlife, the flooded meadows providing winter homes for migrant swans, ducks, geese and waders. It is the most important breeding site in southwest England for waterfowl. Increasingly rare species, such as king-fishers, woodpeckers, bitterns and nightjars are also found here.

The threat to the Somerset Levels has come from two sources: river canalization and pump drainage schemes. Canalization straightens out the water course, replaces banks with levées and, courtesy of the ubiquitous JCB, turns an ecologically rich river bank into a sterile dyke. Pump drainage schemes lower the water table and control the

TO THE FARMER THIS LOOKS AN UNTIDY MESS;
TO THE NATURALIST IT IS A RARE AND IMPORTANT
HABITAT. THE SOMERSET LEVELS

flow of water along the rivers. They enable the grassland regime to be 'improved' – or replaced altogether by cereals and other field crops. The ecological effects of both processes are far-reaching. Wild flowers are virtually eliminated from the meadows and severely reduced along the water courses. Both breeding and migrant birds are forced out. High applications of chemicals pose a devastating threat to fields and drainage ditches alike. The Somerset Levels, left to the devices of the water authorities and the farmers, would become yet another sterile prairie.

In 1978, one of the Levels, the 130 acres of West Sedgemoor, 7 miles east of Taunton, was faced with just such a prospect. Two local farmers applied to the Ministry of Agriculture to help finance the installation of their own pump-drainage scheme on 44 acres of West Sedgemoor. This in itself may seem trivial, but it represented one-third of this particular Level, which in turn provided a refuge for 80 per cent of the wildlife species present on the Levels as a whole. Since by now only 10 per cent of the Levels were unaffected by pump drainage – providing a refuge for the wildlife driven out from elsewhere – it was decided that a stand had to be taken. As far as the conservation lobby was concerned, enough was enough.

The farming regime on West Sedgemoor was a low input/low output system given over to summer grazing and haymaking. Regular winter flooding was tolerated since the Moor was virtually unused at that time of the year. Apart from dairying the only other activity was willow growing for basket-making and charcoal. Although it is manmade, West Sedgemoor supported a wide variety of plant and animal life, but these in turn were dependent upon the continuation of the local tradition of farming practice. So the scene was set by the late 1970s for what was to become a classic confrontation between farming and conservation interests.

As on Exmoor local organizations were sponsored by powerful governmental backers. The Wessex Water Authority, which was responsible for drainage, was grant-aided by the Ministry of Agriculture, as were local farmers. In the opposing camp stood the Somerset Trust for Nature Conservation, in turn supported by the Nature Conservancy Council and, ultimately, the Department of the Environment. Other conservation bodies, such as the Royal Society for the Protection of Birds, were also involved, but it was the NCC which acted as cheerleader – or ringleader, depending on one's view – in the Somerset Levels. In 1973, following reorganization, the NCC had taken on the role of general ecological 'watchdog' and disseminator of information on nature conservation, a role roughly parallel to that of the Countryside Commission on landscapes and recreation. The NCC, formerly the Nature

THE CLASSIC SOMERSET LEVELS LANDSCAPE – RETAINED
ONLY BY CAREFUL AND SENSITIVE MANAGEMENT

'AN APPARENTLY TIMELESS AND TRANQUIL OASIS. . .'

Conservancy, was created by the same Act of 1949 that established the National Parks (see Chapter 4). It was responsible for identifying and designating National Nature Reserves (NNRs) and local Sites of Special Scientific Interest (SSSIs). There are now sixty-five NNRs and over 3000 SSSIs. The aim has been to preserve a cross-section of the most interesting ecological communities or geological sections and to protect areas of particularly rich habitats or rare species of plants and animals. West Sedgemoor certainly fell into this category.

The purpose of designation was to protect wildlife from the threat of destruction. In practice the NCC was often powerless to intervene, having few staff and limited resources. It was aware that agricultural change was threatening many SSSIs, but lacked the means to monitor, let alone prevent it. West Sedgemoor, for example, was not even on a list of Britain's most important conservation sites which the NCC produced in 1977, mainly because it was unaware of the wealth of wildlife on the Levels. Aware of its weakness, the NCC was prepared to make a stand on Sedgemoor and attempt, once and for all, to place effective controls on the direction of agricultural change.

The NCC began by conducting a consultation exercise which listed a number of possible options for land use on the Levels. The published consultation paper went swiftly to the crux of the problem. 'The fundamental question', it concluded, 'is how a meaningful strategy could work on the Somerset Levels without sacrifice of the freedom of the individual owner to farm his land as he wishes.' How indeed? There was already evidence of polarized opinions over precisely this issue. From then on the pace of the conflict hotted up. First the NCC decided, somewhat belatedly, that the Levels in general and West Sedgemoor in particular deserved designation as an SSSI. From 1977 onwards this meant that applications to the Ministry of Agriculture for grant aid for, say, drainage schemes, were being informally referred to the NCC prior to a decision being made. At this point the NFU and the CLA began to take an interest in what was going on. Then in August 1978, the NCC decided to send a standard consultation letter to local farmers and landowners indicating its intention formally to designate West Sedgemoor as an SSSI. A map was enclosed with the letter indicating the extent of the site, together with some indication of what designation would mean in practice. The blue touch-paper was well and truly lit.

For the next three years the temperature was raised still further as the NCC was drawn into frequent confrontation with the Ministry of Agriculture over grant applications. West Sedgemoor's 44 acres became, like the Critical Amenity Area on Exmoor discussed in Chapter 4, a virility symbol for the farming and conservation

lobbies. Local farmers and conservationists engaged in a good deal of 'grandstanding' for their respective national audiences and supporters. What was at stake was the very designation process itself – who should decide where SSSIs were to be and how were associated management agreements to take account of the possible impact on land values (or 'conservation blight' as the NFU preferred to call it). Just to add to the temptation to posture, after 1981 West Sedgemoor also became a test case for the implementation of the Wildlife and Countryside Act, the government's attempt to reconcile the claims of agriculture and conservation on the British countryside.

——— THE WILDLIFE AND COUNTRYSIDE ACT ———

The road from Exmoor to West Sedgemoor ran via Whitehall and Westminster. The conflict on Exmoor led, after some delay, to the Wildlife and Countryside Act of 1981, which enshrined a voluntary approach to conservation. The aim was to encourage management agreements among farmers and landowners rather than rely heavily on compulsory control. The act's passage through parliament had been difficult, attracting 2300 proposed amendments. At the heart of the controversy lay the establishment of procedures to safeguard wildlife habitats. The government initially proposed to protect only a small number of SSSIs from agricultural development. The conservation groups demanded protection for all 3500, suggesting that owners should be *obliged* to notify the NCC of any proposed change and negotiate a management agreement. Where a reasonable agreement proved impossible the NCC should be given reserve powers of compulsion. But the NCC itself was not entirely happy about this, fearing constant confrontation with farmers and lacking the resources to police the system.

In the end the principle of voluntary agreement remained the key to the act. It set out procedures whereby the Ministry of Agriculture, when considering applications for improvement grants inside the National Parks, SSSIs and other specified areas, should take conservation matters into account. Furthermore, when an agricultural grant was refused on conservation grounds, the objecting authority (the NCC in SSSIs, the county planning authority in National Parks) would be required to offer a compensation payment to the farmer. The farming lobby regarded this as fair recompense for designation; conservationists, on the other hand, were appalled. If the Exmoor precedent was anything to go by, wildlife and landscape protection was destined to become an expensive business. Much would depend on the precedents set by the first few cases under the act. Even after the act was passed a code of practice for

owners of SSSIs had still to be worked out. Moreover, financial guidelines still had to be drawn up for compensating farmers denied an agricultural improvement grant.

So the stakes in West Sedgemoor were high when, at the beginning of 1982 an already fraught situation was thrust forward into the national spotlight as a test-bed for the new legislation. The NCC opened the bidding with a proposal to designate 1000 hectares (2400 acres) of West Sedgemoor as an SSSI. Its letter to local farmers included a long list of farming operations (drawn up by NCC central office to cover all eventualities) which could be controlled. This immediately gave the NCC a reputation among local farmers for rampant bureaucracy. The CLA countered with a proposal for 500 hectares and the Ministry of Agriculture proposed 370. The NFU, meanwhile, dragged its feet during the period of statutory consultation, awaiting the publication of financial guidelines and hoping that the NCC would not be able to afford extensive designation. But the NCC held its ground and in Octobeer 1982 reconfirmed its original proposal.

Feelings then ran very high. Political pressure was brought to bear on the NCC and in the following January its chairman, Sir Ralph Verney, was not reappointed. In February NCC officials and local conservationists were burned in effigy by angry farmers. It took a ministerial visit in March and a promise of adequate compensation to bring a degree of calm to this torrid affair. A new district valuer was brought in and after seven months thirty agreements had been initiated, with compensation agreed at around £70–£90 per acre – or around £150,000 per annum at 1983 prices for the whole of West Sedgemoor and over £1 million for the remainder of the Somerset Levels. At this rate it would have been cheaper for the NCC to buy it.

If this was a foretaste of things to come there were few observers who were prepared to believe that the Wildlife and Countryside Act was an adequate solution to the conflict between farming and conservation. If this scale of brinkmanship, civil disorder and expense occurred every time a farmer threatened to plough up an SSSI then the act would be unworkable. It hardly seemed a sufficiently robust piece of legislation to protect the countryside. The 'Battle of Sedgemoor' came to centre around the authority of the NCC itself and whether it was capable, financially, and politically, of standing up to powerful farming interests. In the end the NCC did so – but only just. The cost took the form of unprecedented assurances to farmers and landowners. Henceforward an unscrupulous farmer in possession of an SSSI had only to *threaten* to affect it by changing his pattern of management in order to receive *guaranteed* levels of compensation which removed much of the risk from his farming

business. In effect a pistol could be held at the head of the NCC which would somehow have to find the resources to protect precious sites.

At least the NCC was granted large increases in its budget in order to meet its responsibilities under the act. Perhaps this was just as well, for the NCC had to embark upon the mammoth task of renotifying the 40,000 or so owners of existing SSSIs and negotiate agreements with around one-third of them. The cost was estimated at £15 million per year. Progress has been understandably slow – by March 1986 362 management agreements had been negotiated at an annual cost of £2 million. A review of the act by independent consultants in 1985 concluded that the annual cost of compensation plus administration could go as high as £31 million, plus £52 million in lump-sum payments. There have been some widely-publicized examples of landowners being paid many hundreds of thousands of pounds for not undertaking agricultural improvements in sensitive areas which they would hardly have contemplated without the prospect of grant aid from the Ministry of Agriculture. The simple process of renotification has triggered off demands for compensation in one-third of the cases.

It remains to be seen how long the present unsatisfactory situation will last. At times it is difficult to avoid the conclusion that all the parties concerned recognize the act as only an interim measure and that a good deal of jostling for position is therefore going on in order to take advantage of the next piece of legislation in this area. The longer-term consequences of the furore which surrounded the passage of the act are likely to be more far-reaching, however. First, the issue of wildlife conservation became intensively politicized. Central government was forced to take a hand. The Wildlife and Countryside Act may, in the view of many, have been an unsatisfactory outcome, but the fact that legislation was deemed necessary at all was highly significant. Second, it became clear that the previously unquestioned belief that farmers were the trusted custodians of the countryside now lay in tatters. The publicity which surrounded the battles on Exmoor, West Sedgemoor, Halvergate and elsewhere did little for farming's image as the steward of Britain's rural heritage. By 1984 both the NFU and the CLA seemed to realize this. Both organizations produced policy documents on farming and conservation which went some way towards agreeing on the need to alleviate the problem. They also began to discern that there might be money in conservation.

The one point on which all sides were agreed was that matters could not go on like this. The conservation lobby realized that it was confined to dealing with the bruise rather than the fist. The proper conservation of the countryside could only be attained

POLLARDED WILLOWS STRETCHING TO THE HORIZON. . .
THE LOST WORLD OF THE SOMERSET LEVELS

by gaining influence over the direction of agricultural policy. Similarly the farming industry began to realize that environmentalism was not merely the passing fad of a few cranks which would eventually fade away. The introduction of Environmentally Sensitive Areas (see Chapter 4) – of which West Sedgemoor was one – recognized that farming support could be made more environmentally responsible without recourse to the bluff and bluster of Exmoor, Halvergate and the Somerset Levels. The battle moved away from the defence of particular sites to the corridors of power, where a determined attempt was undertaken to effect the greening of agricultural policy.

FUTURE PROSPECTS

In years to come it may be possible to see the Wildlife and Countryside Act as the last example of an essentially outdated reactive and defensive approach to the conservation of wildlife and landscapes. Certainly if one was constructing a rational policy to integrate agricultural production and environmental conservation one would not start from here. Environmentalists do not feel that the countryside is safeguarded by current legislation. Outside designated sites farming proceeds largely unfettered by environmental concerns and even within designated areas controls have only limited effectiveness. Farmers, on the other hand, fear the interference of a remote and ignorant bureaucracy which ties up essential farming operations in a knot of red tape.

And yet there is no *necessary* conflict between profitable farming, the maintenance of desirable landscapes and the sustaining of a diverse range of wildlife habitats. The fact that farmers today use twelve times the amount of pesticides that they did at the end of the war is not the result of some inevitable law of scientific progress. Changes can be made. As Chapter 2 made clear the revolution in agricultural production has now been achieved. The pressure on farmers to intensify further ought no longer to be there. We no longer require a further increase in food production when so much is already surplus to our needs. In practice, however, farmers still feel the need to intensify in order to survive. Perhaps farmers can be offered incentives to conserve the environment via farm support policies, rather than compelled to do so via the planning system?

This philosophy lies behind the current rather timorous attempt to introduce ESAs. In such a heavily state supported and administered industry as agriculture the apparatus exists to bring about a redirection. The tentacles of agricultural support, advice and education reach out far into the countryside. Only the political will seems missing to overcome the inherent – but sometimes understandable – suspicion of the

farmers themselves. It is not beyond the wit of this huge apparatus to swing behind a modified set of aims and objectives. Farm business plans are already required as a prerequisite of much grant-aid: why cannot farm plans also incorporate clearly stated conservation objectives? Rather than be offered compensation for something which they never received in the first place, farmers should be offered a more balanced portfolio of incentives from the public purse.

Conservation is an issue which is not going to disappear. To believe otherwise would be to ignore the *social* transformation of rural Britain which was outlined in Chapter 3. Much of the political force of the environmental movement stems from the ex-urban newcomers now living in the countryside who, as we have seen, have done so much to change the character of rural life. It is they who are in the vanguard of opposition to modern farming methods and who are staunch defenders of traditional landscapes and wildlife habitats. In their sincere desire to preserve and protect there may be more than a whiff of Arcadian sentiment and good old-fashioned self-interest, but they are a political force to be reckoned with. There may be 180,000 farmers, but there are 3 million members of conservation groups. Many are influential and articulate: they will not be fobbed off with reassuring platitudes.

The environmental lobby is not always as far-sighted as it wishes to believe. Rushing from site to site in order to engage in environmental fire-fighting has been very necessary, but hardly conducive to long-term strategic thinking. It is only very recently that alternative farming policies have been spelt out in detail. Even now, other, equally pressing rural problems remain overlooked. The environmental lobby is, for example, peculiarly myopic about the broader social and economic future of the countryside. In 1986 this was vividly illustrated in a notable episode on the Inner Hebridean island of Islay. The local peat bog is a feeding ground for migrant geese, indeed one of the most important in Europe. But the peat is also needed to flavour Islay's renowned malt whisky. The local distillery's application to extend peat cutting and reduce the available space for the geese provoked protests from a number of environmental groups. Two distinguished conservationists, Jonathan Porritt and David Bellamy, visited Islay in order to convince the local inhabitants of the conservationist case. They were run off the island by a population which put jobs before geese.

The significance of this lay not so much in the particulars of the case, as in demonstrating the trap into which many environmental groups have fallen. They have not developed a social and economic strategy for the countryside to anything like the same extent that they have developed conservation strategy, or even a critique of

'. . .EXQUISITELY PRESERVED IN A TIME-CAPSULE. . .'.
LOWER KINGCOMBE, DORSET

agriculture. There is no necessary conflict between economic growth and conservation, any more than there is a necessary conflict between agriculture and conservation. Perhaps the greatest tragedy of the long series of disputes which preceded and followed the passage of the Wildlife and Countryside Act is the extent to which environmental issues have come to dominate public debate about the future of the countryside. Meanwhile, other, equally important, issues have been obscured. When more public attention is given to, say, the extinction of the Large Blue butterfly than to the economic well-being of the rural population then the time has come to be concerned.

Today it sometimes seems that more attention is given to the effect of pesticides on butterflies than on farm workers, or that the only endangered species in the countryside are of a non-human kind. More concern has now been expressed over how to preserve the countryside than how to allow it to develop in ways which benefit the whole spectrum of the rural population. This is not to argue for some kind of environmental philistinism. It is not, in any case, a question of conservation *versus* community development, but of how the two can be brought together. For the countryside must be allowed to change and develop if it is to sustain a viable social balance – and thus an attractive and ecologically rewarding landscape – at all. Rigid protectionism has its place as a last resort, but conservation has to be a thread which runs through all aspects of the social and economic well-being of the countryside.

Let us examine the effects of misguided protectionism in practice. In a hidden valley west of Dorchester in Dorset there lies the Lower Kingcombe estate. Until the summer of 1987 it had remained virtually unchanged for centuries, thanks to the eccentricities of successive owners. Field patterns had remained for four centuries, the meadows intact and unsprayed. It gave a tantalizing glimpse of what the landscape of southern England would have looked like had the post-war agricultural revolution not taken place. The meadows are a glorious blaze of wild flowers, surrounded by mature trees and hedgerows, all folded into a valley through which runs a gurgling trout stream. If anywhere in England is Arcadia it must be here. Protected by a fortunate quirk of ownership (and recently – and more prosaically – by SSSI designation) Lower Kingcombe has been exquisitely preserved in a time capsule.

The only problem is: it is virtually deserted. The local hamlet is derelict. Windowless and roofless, none of the houses have been inhabited for some time. Countryside like this can no longer sustain a working population with an adequate standard of living which the rest of us would take for granted. Ultimately the

ENVIRONMENTALLY RICH, BUT SOCIALLY, AND ECONOMICALLY, DEAD:
LOWER KINGCOMBE, DORSET

countryside is not just a collection of landscapes and wildlife habitats, but an environment in which people live and work. In recent years this has been overlooked. A countryside which is not allowed to develop is a countryside which is condemned to being socially and economically in decline.

In Lower Kingcombe the countryside is beautifully preserved, but as a society it is dead. As it happened, in May 1987 the estate was sold off as separate lots. In the lanes outside the derelict cottages purchasers could be viewed stooped over the bonnets of their Volvos inspecting their architects' plans. Whatever Lower Kingcombe is to become, it is unlikely to be the kind of rural community it might have been had its development been handled more sensitively. The countryside should not be allowed to become merely a museum of our Arcadian past, or an object of polite observation as we relax from the serious business of improving *our* living standards. In this, at least, the lesson to be drawn from Lower Kingcombe is clear.

No one wishes to see the destruction of our countryside. Who could possibly be in favour of such a thing? But we must introduce into the debate about the future of the countryside more of a balance between conservation and community development, between the necessary desire to preserve our landscapes and wildlife while attending the needs of the people who work there. Perhaps as a nation we have become so separated from the reality of rural life that we can *only* relate to it as a landscape or as a nature reserve. Certainly, as we shall see in the next chapter, visiting and observing the countryside, as opposed to working in it, has never been more popular.

'. . .A MUSEUM OF OUR ARCADIAN PAST. . .'?

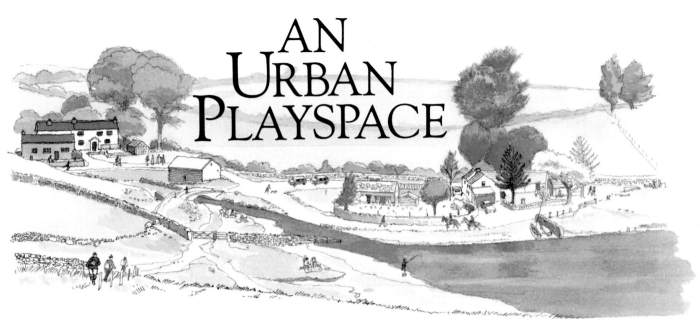

AN URBAN PLAYSPACE

If you are looking for some peace and quiet on a Bank Holiday or a summer's weekend the countryside is not necessarily the best place to go. On a typical summer Sunday about 18 million of us can be found there, hoping to 'get away from it all'. But getting away from it all is often moreedifficult than it seems. Having struggled through the traffic jams and found a suitable parking space where is the harassed visitor to go? For the countryside is private property, not an extended municipal park, and the right of public access is restricted. Those wishing to get away from it all might more easily find a place to relax in the peace and quiet of the city centre.

The public is demanding access to the countryside for recreation and leisure in ever-increasing numbers. Farmers and landowners are, however, understandably somewhat nervous about this. On an individual basis, the farmer will often welcome the interested and respectful visitor. Many farmers, after all, cater for tourists and daytrippers by offering bed and breakfast accommodation, camp sites, outdoor recreation facilities and so on. But when visitors to the countryside are considered *en masse*, then the farmer's traditional nervousness towards the urban population begins to take over. In moments of mature reflection the farmer may pity the 'townie' – a pity based upon the farmer's assessment of the quality of inner-city life – but that genuine twinge of concern is easily swept aside by the nightmare of being 'invaded', 'swamped' or 'overrun' by a 'mass' of 'ignorant' daytrippers and holiday-makers.

Some of these fears have been forged out of bitter experience. The public retains a sense of the countryside being theirs to roam around, even though most of it is privately owned. People view it as a kind of vast urban playspace across which it is possible to walk their dogs, hike with their friends, ride their ponies or merely look at

the view. Many are aware of the Country Code – the list of do's and dont's concerning open gates, litter, the control of dogs, fire risks and so on – but many are not. Fewer still are aware of the Access Code – the brief summary of the legal rights and obligations over public access to the countryside published by the Countryside Commission. Eighteen million people are bound to contain a fair proportion of the thoughtless and the ignorant, even if those who are downright malicious form only a tiny minority.

Modern hi-tech farming has also made agriculture even more incompatible with uncontrolled recreation. Intensive livestock operations increase the susceptibility of animals to diseases easily spread by humans, and visitors threaten good farm hygiene. The danger can be easily reversed – some farming operations, particularly spraying, threaten visitors. So farmers may object to visitors 'roaming all over' their land and will point out with some vehemence that they would not expect the same licence to wander around urban factories. For the exasperated farmer who fears for the future of his pig unit or his broiler house, or for the cereals farmer who does not take kindly to his best malting barley being trampled down in order to make an impromptu picnic site, the simplest solution is to go in for siege tactics. Up will go the 'Trespassers Will Be Prosecuted' and 'Keep Out' signs, the extra barbed wire is ordered and the shotgun is cleaned and prepared. Footpaths may suddenly disappear under the plough or new fences are erected across them. Signposts mysteriously vanish and perhaps an unsociable bull is posted in a strategically sited field. The battle lines are drawn to repel the massed hordes of urban denizens.

FREEDOM TO ROAM

Such obstructive behaviour has traditionally provoked an equally strong public response, however. We can all draw upon a deep folk memory, going back before the enclosures, which tells us that, whatever the law may say, the public has a right to roam the countryside. Legally this is far from being the case, but there has always been a strongly-held view that the countryside is 'ours', not 'theirs', that fundamentally it belongs to the nation as a whole, not to the few individuals who might be temporarily in possession.

The demand for a public 'freedom to roam' has been a powerful, though intermittent, voice pitched against the entrenched legal privileges of landowners. As early as the 1820s footpath preservation societies were formed in several cities in

northern England and at the end of the nineteenth century a successful campaign preserved a number of urban commons in London for public recreation. Britain's first conservation group, the Commons, Open Spaces and Footpaths Preservation Society, was founded as long ago as 1865. A number of these early groups survived, federated and subsequently formed themselves into the Ramblers Association.

It was between the wars that the modern access movement came to maturity. There were, however, distinct regional variations in its character. In the south of England a more affluent Home Counties middle class began to 'consume' the countryside in increasing numbers. As we saw in Chapter 3, the countryside was becoming more accessible due to suburban growth and increasing car ownership. Suburban residents began to explore their rural hinterland. Knowledgeable about the aesthetics of landscapes, the longevity of rustic traditions and the value of the natural environment, they were often woefully ignorant about the realities of agriculture and the economics of rural life. In part this was because their rural sensibilities were culled almost entirely from books: the cultured urbanite was inundated with guide books, rural reminiscences and interpretive texts which defined the rural world for them. In this respect, at least, not much has changed. Accessibility by car reduced the countryside to a series of medieval churches, cream teas and quaint rustic features.

As the popularity of visiting the countryside grew, so did the alarm of those who wished to preserve its peace and quiet. When the CPRE was formed in 1926 (see Chapter 3) it was already apparent that a dilemma existed between promoting the spiritual pleasures of the countryside and protecting it from the 'madding crowds' of Morris owners. Cultural elitism was never far from the surface here. To be sure the countryside needed to be preserved for 'the nation', but it also needed to be protected *from* 'the public'. Only a self-appointed minority possessed the enlightenment needed to appreciate the countryside fully. They could enthuse lyrically about a Norman arch, but miss entirely the bleak realities of agriculture in the midst of depression. Stella Gibbon's devastating satire, *Cold Comfort Farm* (published in 1932), parodied brilliantly such Hampstead-based perceptions, but they were to be a powerful force in the moves to establish a public right of access to the countryside.

If 'going for a spin' around the leafy lanes of the Home Counties provides one image of public interest in the countryside between the wars, another is the bare-kneed and rucksacked hiker setting out to commune with Nature on downland or fell. In the south of England such a pursuit could take advantage of the dense network of ancient footpaths and bridleways which criss-crossed areas like the Downs and Chilterns. In

THE OVER-USE OF THE COUNTRYSIDE CAN LEAD TO PROBLEMS WITH EROSION:
NEAR LULWORTH, DORSET

the north access to the open countryside was not so easy. Northern cities like Manchester and Sheffield were surrounded by the beautiful open moorland of the Peak District, but it was rendered virtually inaccessible by the restrictive property rights of local land-owners, anxious to allow their grouse to remain undisturbed and buttressed by a fear-some army of gamekeepers determined to keep the urban citizenry at bay.

As early as 1876 the Hayfield and Kinder Scout Ancient Footpaths Association had been founded to oppose path closures in the area. It was part of the movement to establish the freedom to roam at will across the open spaces of the uplands. In 1884 this right was gained for Scotland, but a Private Members Bill introduced in 1888 to extend the right to England and Wales was defeated. By the mid 1920s rock-climbing, 'bog-trotting' and

rambling had grown to the proportions of a 'craze'. On summer weekends up to 10,000 ramblers could be found using the Peak District. Demands for the freedom to roam grew. From 1926 an annual rally was held at Winnats Pass, near Castleton in Derbyshire. Unlike the southern-based campaign, this was a radical and largely working-class movement. By the 1930s it began to focus on the issue of private property rights, leading the access movement to acquire overtones of class warfare.

From then on the access movement thrived on a heady mixture of Romantic sentiment and hard-nosed class politics (which attracted the interest of the Communist Party). Unemployed people were recruited into the radical British Workers' Sports Federation and the Ramblers' Rights Movement. Support was canvassed for mass trespass as a means of gaining public attention. The most famous of these occurred on Sunday, 24 April 1932 when several hundred ramblers invaded Kinder Scout. A stage-managed mass trespass of the Duke of Devonshire's grouse moors, following a rally nearby, led to scuffles between ramblers and estate wardens, immortalized in the tabloid press as 'Wild Scenes at Kinder Scout'. It was an event which was to pass into the folklore of the rambling movement. Six of the ringleaders were arrested and five subsequently convicted and sentenced to prison terms of between two and six months. Further outbreaks of direct action followed, though without scenes of violence. In one respect at least mass trespass had been successful: public access to the countryside was now placed firmly on the political agenda.

A limited Access to the Mountains Act was introduced in 1939, but it was not until after the Second World War that real progress was made. In 1949 the National Parks and Access to the Countryside Act not only set up the National Parks but regulated public access. The act did not go as far as offering a legal right of access to open and uncultivated land, but it did enable local authorities to negotiate Access Agreements with landowners. In the last resort the act also empowered the local authority to make a compulsory Access Order. In practice access agreements were widely used only in the Peak District and access orders were seldom resorted to anywhere. The act did, however, adopt a more positive approach to rights of way, requiring county councils to survey their areas and produce 'definitive maps' of footpaths, bridleways and other rights of way. This, too, has been a slow and unsatisfactory process, still not complete when the Wildlife and Countryside Act of 1981 altered the system. Rather more successful has been the establishment of a network of long-distance footpaths, which the act also enabled. The first of these, perhaps appropriately, was the Pennine Way which runs northwards for 250 miles from Edale, in the lea of Kinder Scout.

—— MANAGING PUBLIC ACCESS ——

By the 1960s, as car ownership spread and leisure time increased, planners and conservationists were beginning to find common cause with farmers and landowners over fears about the countryside being overrun by visitors. Although the ramblers and cyclists who populated the access lobby in the 1930s liked to depict themselves as a 'mass movement', they depended for their success on organization rather than numbers. Now countryside recreation took on a much wider mass appeal. The most immediate sign of this was the growth in so-called informal recreation – countryside trips in cars, usually incorporating picnics, visits to ancient monuments or short walks.

For those concerned about protecting the countryside the initial response was a negative and defensive one. Growing public interest in the countryside was somehow seen as a problem which had to be contained. Those who 'appreciated' the countryside were anxious that others should not 'spoil' it for them. Even those sympathetic to the 'freedom to roam' became alarmed when more and more of the public took them at their word. Concern grew for fragile landscapes and vulnerable wildlife habitats placed at risk by the wave of tramping feet. The fear of 'access in excess' became more pronounced and increasing emphasis was placed on intercepting, channelling and guiding visitors away from unspoilt areas. In so far as this involved finding ingenious ways of keeping as many people as possible away from pristine parts of rural Britain, then alliances began to be forged between farmers, conservationists and village newcomers, each, in their own way, fearful of what unrestricted access might bring in its wake.

The organization which found itself coping with this somewhat difficult situation was the Countryside Commission, which, after 1968, had general responsibilities for both conservation *and* recreation (see Chapter 4). Although it operated out of a converted police station in Cheltenham, the Countryside Commission lacked executive powers. It could only educate, inform, urge and demonstrate by example what could be achieved. It did, however, have the ability to grant-aid schemes proposed and administered by local authorities and the private sector, and this gave it some leverage over access provision. In only a few areas, such as nature reserves, did access policy favour the deliberate rationing or restriction of public entry – whether by toll, permit or membership of a club or society. In general the Countryside Commission proceeded on the basis of a two-tier system of channelling 'passive', car-borne, urban visitors into deliberately contrived 'honeypots' or urban fringe 'buffers', leaving the remoter areas 'unspoilt' for 'serious' wilderness seekers.

LULWORTH COVE, DORSET: INFAMOUS FOR THE PRESSURE
WHICH THOUSANDS OF VISITORS CREATE EACH YEAR

This policy remains an important element in countryside recreation management. It is a subtle form of restriction which proceeds by a philosophy akin to apartheid. Environmental bantustans are set aside where virtually unrestricted leisure activity is allowed and even encouraged via the provision of recreation facilities. This enables access to the remaining areas to be rationed for those interested in a more solitary appreciation of the countryside, even to the extent that reaching such areas may be made deliberately difficult. Rural honeypots take a variety of forms. In some areas they are brought about by planning policies and associated restrictions on development control. Thus Bowness-on-Windermere is sacrificed for the greater good of the Lake District. Matlock Bath is allowed its range of kiss-me-quick attractions to keep its devotees away from the Peak District. The intention is to use such inland resorts to relieve the pressure for recreational development elsewhere in the countryside.

Other, more positive forms of honeypot planning have been developed. The most ambitious have been country parks, created and administered by local authorities, but grant-aided by the Countryside Commission. They have allowed an expansion of choice for the public interested in visiting the countryside, but are often deliberately located on urban-fringe sites in order to act as 'buffers' to the rural areas beyond. In practice country parks have often conformed fairly closely to the notion of an urban municipal park, but they have also brought the countryside to the urban dweller by providing them with a staged version of rural life – farm museums, craft exhibitions, and even working farms where visitors may observe farming operations like milking or shearing. Private enterprise has also seized the opportunity, opening up a range of facilities running from modern commercial farms thrown open to the public to theme parks, following the American model, which have no particular rural connection.

Other facilities have been more modest, such as the provision of picnic sites, public toilets and car-parking facilities (known in the trade as 'a view with a loo'). In each case

SHOWING THE WAY:
THE COUNTRYSIDE MUST BE MANAGED FOR ACCESS

the intention has been to combine, however uneasily, the encouragement of public recreation in the countryside (on the grounds that it is Good for You) with the necessity of protecting its attractive qualities and reassuring farming and environmental interests. Even the long-distance footpaths occasionally fall into this category. By providing an adequate infrastructure of signs, stiles, accommodation, etc. and imaginative marketing, visitor pressure is removed from rights of way which do not have the same carrying capacity.

These developments, while often worthy in themselves, are a far cry from 'freedom to roam'. Planning for them drew heavily upon the theories of traffic engineers and was based on somewhat simplistic views of supply and demand. Little effort was made to ascertain the attitudes, preferences and motivations of those who visit the countryside. But at least facilities were provided – over 200 country parks and 240 picnic sites in the public sector alone. On the other hand little was done to increase the opportunities for rural recreation among the more deprived sections of the urban population. Consequently most visitors to the countryside continue to come from a fairly circumscribed group of affluent, car-owning, suburban families, while those arguably in greater need are scarcely catered for. But again, there is ambivalence over whether they *should* be catered for: to the farmer and the conservationist alike a vision is conjured up of marauding inner-city teenagers and other undesirable aliens, wreaking havoc in the tranquillity of rural Britain best kept away from 'those kinds of people'.

To many of us the idea that leisure pursuits in the countryside should be managed in this way is rather depressing. We tend to go to the countryside in order to get away from being 'managed'. And it has to be admitted that a mild deception is sometimes involved. Many rural honeypots, in the best Disneyland tradition, hold up to the urban visitor the image of bucolic rural life which they expect to see. They often reinforce the public's perception of rural life as traditional and unchanging – a kind of basket-weaving and blacksmiths image – which bears little relationship to the reality of the modern rural world. Well-meaning attempts to educate the public by these means often end up obscuring as much as clarifying our understanding of rural life. The risk is that the same misinformation which led Stella Gibbon to reach for her pen is being perpetuated by a mixture of commercial necessity (there's money in nostalgia) and effective modern methods of marketing and presentation. By increasing the provision of rural leisure facilities and expanding the range of choice, honeypots like country parks have been a welcome development, but how far they have genuinely improved public understanding of the countryside is open to question.

VISITORS TO THE COUNTRYSIDE ARE A VARIED GROUP: RIVER WEY, SURREY

Fortunately, recent countryside management policies are based on a rather more sophisticated understanding of the demands of visitors and are often much more unobtrusive in the ways in which they manage access. Some, at least, of the fears of the countryside being destroyed by masses of visitors have now been dispelled. The well-publicized cases of overcrowding and ecological damage in the Lake District, parts of the Derbyshire Peak District or on the Downs in Kent and Sussex are localized and somewhat untypical. It is possible, for example, to recall the fears expressed in Devon and Somerset during the construction of the M5 beyond Bristol at the prospect of hundreds of thousands of daytrippers from Birmingham and the Black Country descending upon Exmoor and Dartmoor. In the event the vast majority continued to make for the seaside resorts in the area, leaving local conservationists to fend off the more immediate threats from farmers and water authorities.

The unspoken assumption here, as so often elsewhere, was that crowds would impair enjoyment. Since the founding of the National Trust and the CPRE leaders of conservation organizations have tended to take it for granted that the enjoyment of the countryside is an essentially solitary experience: Wordsworth has a lot to answer for. In fact it is a preference which exists predominantly among the middle aged and the middle class. Common observation suggests that other social groups enjoy the conviviality of being part of a crowd and find open spaces 'with nothing to do' dead and unappealing. Countryside Commission statistics even suggest that the overwhelming majority of visitors venture no more than a couple of hundred yards from their car. Just as many rural inhabitants feel bewildered by the street life of the city, so many urban dwellers retain similar anxieties about the unknown world of the countryside.

Most people using farmland for recreation are not, in any case, visitors who have journeyed many miles from the urban centres of population. Instead most are – not surprisingly when one thinks about it – local inhabitants taking short walks for exercise and relaxation. What they want are clearly marked and unobstructed footpaths. Since many of them are newcomers to the local village, they share the desire of farmers and others to protect the countryside from misuse. They do, however, react vehemently to illicit attempts to interfere with their simple pleasures. This suggests that the demands of recreation can be accommodated by much more modest initiatives than appeared likely in the 1960s. In some respect the debate has been sidetracked by the peculiar social blindness which sometimes affects the judgements of the interested parties. The erosion of footpaths often receives more attention than the damage caused by skiing and horseriding; and the siting of

refreshment kiosks and public lavatories creates more anguish than yachting marinas. This may not be unconnected with the typical social profiles of their users.

It would be mistaken to argue that the problems created by the increasing demand for recreation in the countryside are entirely illusory or simply a matter of arbitrary taste: they clearly are not. Nowhere is this more important than on the urban fringe, where access to farmland is most easily gained and is least organized. Here the problems of trespass from neighbouring urban areas can be almost a way of life for affected farmers. Most can offer spine-chilling examples of the havoc caused by damaged machinery, the theft or destruction of farm property, random vandalism to gates, fences and farm buildings, the worrying of livestock and the constant nuisance of fly-tipping and litter. Some of it is malicious, a lot of it is thoughtless, but most of it causes distress and anger. Fortunately it is usually localized in extent, which is of little consolation to the farmers affected, but does suggest that the answer lies in local solutions, rather than generalized measures to protect farmland from public access.

So from the 1970s onwards the emphasis in countryside management began to change. It became more positive in encouraging widespread public access, but also recognized that the needs of the public are many and varied. Relatively few demand the solitude of the rural wilderness; not everyone regards the countryside as being spoiled by organized facilities for visitors; there is often conflict *between* different categories of users. Many potential areas of conflict are amenable to small-scale and essentially local solutions rather than grandiose national policies. Countryside management came to mean unobtrusive and small-scale recreation and conservation projects, which would promote goodwill between the interested parties and would be achieved through voluntary agreements. Such an approach hardly thrust the Countryside Commission into the public limelight, nor made the public aware of how much would be achieved in this way. But as far as reconciling recreation and access with conservation and farming was concerned, it was arguably much more effective.

Countryside management is more in tune with the limited resources available for public bodies during the 1980s. The way was paved from the late 1960s onwards with a number of experimental schemes sponsored by the Countryside Commission. The first was carried out in the Hartsop Valley area of the Lake District, beginning in 1969. A second scheme began in Snowdonia in the following year and the two were known collectively as UMEX 1 – the Upland Management Experiment. The aim was to reconcile the interests of visitors and farmers in the uplands by offering financial encouragement to farmers to carry out small schemes which would improve both the

MOST VISITORS TO THE COUNTRYSIDE SIMPLY WISH
TO WALK THROUGH IT. ALBURY DOWN, SURREY

THE USE OF THE COUNTRYSIDE FOR ACTIVITY SPORTS IS INCREASING:
POT-HOLING IN THE BRECON BEACONS NATIONAL PARK

appearance of the landscape and the opportunities for recreation in the area. UMEX involved the appointment of a project officer who would identify problems and take practical steps to solve them. The experiment was carefully monitored and the results were sufficiently encouraging to be extended in the Lake District to a wider area, this becoming UMEX 2.

Typically UMEX projects involved a programme of minor works – erecting stiles, bridges and gates, repairing walls, fences and footpaths. The aim was both to improve the appearance of the landscape – by repairing stone walls, planting broadleaved trees, etc. – and to regularize access by repairing stiles, maintaining signs and keeping paths in good repair. Early results suggested that, with a modicum of goodwill and an energetic and diplomatic project officer, much of the conflict between visitors and farmers over access could be defused. Proper maintenance of rights of way and signposts reduced trespass while encouraging use. Public access could be properly planned and implemented, while farmers were relieved of some of the burden of maintaining the appearance of their land. It was a method of operating which was to be extended to other areas – to the urban fringe (UFEX) around Manchester and North London, to the heritage coasts and to a few AONBs. In 1981, the urban fringe schemes were partially 'privatized' through the creation of the Operation Ground-work which now, through a mix of public and private funding, organizes environmental improvement schemes on the edge of a number of towns and cities.

The experimental phase of UMEX ended in 1976. But it was sufficiently successful to be absorbed into the national park administration in the Lake District whereupon it became the Upland Management Service (UMAS). Similar schemes are run by other National Park authorities. They have been instrumental in changing the attitudes of farmers not only towards visitors, but to the National Park administration itself.

GETTING AWAY FROM IT ALL –
BUT ENTHRALLED BY THE LANDSCAPE?

They have provided local employment and, perhaps more than any other initiative, have brought local farmers into frequent contact with what had previously been regarded as a remote bureaucracy. Countryside management has not been a panacea. It cannot hope to be comprehensive, nor to solve some of the deep-seated social and economic problems which lie behind the neatly trimmed landscapes. But schemes like these have brought about a measurable improvement.

—— UPLAND MANAGEMENT ON THE GROUND ——

If anywhere exemplifies the success of countryside management it is the Lake District. Not only did UMEX begin here, but the Lake District is often held up as an area vulnerable to visitor pressure *par excellence*. The Lake District also exemplified a paradox which lay at the heart of attempts to reconcile recreation, conservation and farming. On the one hand visitor pressure was increasing rapidly, thanks in part to the development of the motorway system; but at the same time agriculture was in decline and the maintenance of the landscape was in jeopardy. One immediate benefit of UMEX to local farmers was that it made a contribution towards the upkeep of their land.

Much of the early work concerned rights of way. A lot of time was spent working with the farming community so that the influx of visitors could be integrated more easily. In practice this meant speeding the visitor through the farmyard and in-bye and out on to the open fell with the minimum of disruption to farming operations: hence the importance of apparently minor works on gates, footpaths, etc. Subsequently the scheme has widened out into landscape conservation work and projects were initiated with farmers to maintain deciduous woodland, keep the drystone walls in good order and maintain other attractive landscape features.

One of the farms which has benefited from this scheme must rank as one of the most visited in Britain. Seathwaite Farm is the Piccadilly Circus of the Lake District footpath network. It lies at the end of a lane which branches off the southern end of Borrowdale, and is the starting point for a number of footpaths which fan out towards Scafell Pike and beyond. During the summer up to 3000 people a day walk through the yard of Seathwaite Farm. Cars, minibuses and caravans may be parked on the approach to the farm for as far back as 2 miles. Most of their occupants demand no more than the solitude of the hills.

The farmer on the receiving end of this crowd of visitors – more than many football league teams would receive on an average Saturday afternoon – is Stanley

WELL-PLANNED FACILITIES ENABLE VISITORS TO
ENJOY THE COUNTRYSIDE WITH THE MINIMUM
OF DISRUPTION: CAMPSITE AT EDALE

Edmondson. He has farmed at Seathwaite all his life so he has become accustomed to dealing with the disruption which such an influx can bring. Somewhat phlegmatically he bows to the inevitable: he fits his farming timetable around the habits of the visitors rather than expecting them to conform to his requirements. Consequently he moves stock before six in the morning so that they do not become mixed up with the traffic outside his farmyard. Having been brought up with the problem he accepts it as a fact of life. He even misses the tourists when they are not around, finding the farm disconcertingly quiet and empty.

Seathwaite Farm is owned by the National Trust. It has not only benefited from UMEX and UMAS, but from the Trust's own efforts to cope with the wear and tear caused by so many visitors. Without maintenance the fellsides would become seriously eroded. Even now deep scars are apparent alongside some of the most popular rights of way. The Trust now employs a full-time maintenance team which undertakes the necessary repairs. During the summer of 1987, for example, the farmyard was being resurfaced with stone setts, while on a fellside nearby the Trust's own 'flying squad' was re-building a heavily eroded path. Signs had been erected and contra-flows were in force: rather like motorway maintenance on the nearby M6.

Seathwaite Farm remains a recognizable working farm in spite of its position. There are some incongruities (not many farmyards can claim to possess public lavatories and a public telephone box), but there are compensations – an outbuilding has been converted into a thriving cafe. The walls are in good repair, unobtrusive but helpful signposts abound, gates have workable catches and the bridge over the beck is sound and robust. The enjoyment of the visitors has not been impaired, while they are discreetly directed through the farm and away on to the fells with the minimum of fuss. The visitor statistics may appal farmers unaccustomed to the problem, but the solutions demonstrably work. Seathwaite remains a viable, working farm, while the breathtaking attractiveness of this part of Borrowdale remains undiminished. What is more the public are able to come and experience it for themselves.

VISITORS: AN ALTERNATIVE CROP?

There are few signs that the public demand for countryside recreation is diminishing. Indeed forms of active recreation which take up more space – like hang-gliding, trail-biking and wind-surfing – have shown a spectacular increase. There is also considerable evidence of latent demand. Farmers who have taken modest steps to

DESPITE THE PRESSURES FROM VISITORS IN THE NATIONAL PARKS,
IT IS STILL POSSIBLE TO GET AWAY FROM IT ALL:
CLAPPER BRIDGE AT POSTBRIDGE IN DARTMOOR

Finding the right mix: quarrying, walking and
picnicking in the Peak District National Park

improve and 'market' the footpaths across their land have been staggered by the public response. What has not yet been established, however, is the role of leisure and recreation in the countryside alongside other major land uses like agriculture and forestry. Should recreation rank alongside food production as an objective of public policy in the countryside? With so much talk of diversification (see Chapter 2) should visitors be regarded as an alternative crop, a source of revenue to compensate for failing farm support?

As a society we have still not worked out the balance we wish to see between farming, conservation and recreation. Countryside management can achieve this at a local level, but it is no substitute for a national strategy. The prospect of a change in the direction of agricultural policy provides an opportunity here, too. It is not beyond the bounds of possibility to bring together a properly planned network of leisure facilities and recreation sites, a scheme for managing and promoting rights of way as a recreational resource and a means of extending the freedom to roam in open country. But all of this presupposes that we assign equal importance to recreation in the countryside as we currently do to food production and are invited to do for conservation.

Given the opportunity and some imaginative planning, the urban population has shown that it is capable of responding and respecting the interests of others. Public demand for more access will not, in any case, go away. Farmers, too, need to understand more about the impulses which prompt the urban dweller to look to the countryside for relaxation and enjoyment. Some of them might, indeed, make money out of them. But landowners will have to concede that, whatever the strict legal interpretation, the public is never going to regard the countryside as something over which it has no rights at all.

With the eventual reform of agricultural policy we must make sure that leisure and recreation are accepted as valid land uses to be incorporated into any strategy for the future of the countryside. It would be a benefit no less important than the improvements in the quality of the environment discussed in the previous two chapters. The public, which foots much of the current bill for agriculture, has a legitimate interest in ensuring that these benefits are achieved. There are also other advantages to be gained, not least from job creation in the countryside and economic gains from promoting further tourist development. If the public's demand for access is seen as an opportunity rather than a threat then, sensitively managed, there could be advantages all round. What, after all, is the point of maintaining the countryside at public expense if the public is denied the opportunity to enjoy it?

WHOSE COUNTRYSIDE?

Here is an everyday story of countryfolk – 1980s style. Micro-Medics is a new and fast-growing company which manufactures computer-based diagnostic systems for doctors. It brings together recent advances in medical science with the very latest forms of computer analysis and database management. It is located, not in the surroundings of a major London teaching hospital, but in a converted stables in a village in Oxfordshire.

This is typical of the kind of economic development which can now be seen taking place all over rural Britain. For the first time since the Industrial Revolution technological change is allowing rural areas to compete on an equal footing with towns and cities for employment. There no longer exists the overriding necessity for manufacturing and services to be in large units close to the major centres of population. Instead new innovations in computing and information technology have allowed growth to take place far away from large urban areas. We are now entering the age of the electronic cottage industry.

ECONOMIC RESTRUCTURING

Over the last decade some profound changes have taken place in the structure of the rural economy, part of the much broader process of economic restructuring which has taken place in Britain as a whole. While inner-city areas have suffered from a massive decline in manufacturing employment, rural areas, especially in the south of England, have experienced considerable growth. Indeed, the fastest growing regions in Britain for manufacturing have been the *rural* areas of south-west England and East Anglia.

they would, on the whole, be moving to higher-paid employment – and good for the nation – because they would be moving into jobs with higher productivity. Circumstances have, however, changed. Much higher levels of unemployment during the 1980s have meant that there are precious few jobs for those displaced by agriculture to go to. Even the benefits to be gained for national productivity have disappeared as agriculture's productivity record has exceeded that of manufacturing industry. So the traditional safety valve which coped with low pay, poor conditions and minimal prospects for advancement within the farming industry has been closed off. Rural workers, who once voted with their feet, now remain trapped as unemployed and underemployed members of the rural community. The presumption of many rural planning authorities that the countryside should be protected from development has scarcely helped their plight.

The need to attract industry into rural areas has been recognized by a number of national and regional bodies which have been set up to provide assistance. The oldest of these is the Development Commission, established as long ago as 1909 to promote economic growth in rural areas. More recently bodies like the Development Board for Mid-Wales, the Highlands and Islands Development Board and the Scottish Development Agency have also promoted economic development within their respective rural areas. Sometimes their efforts have been hampered by unfortunate urban-based assumptions about what constituted 'appropriate' development for rural areas. The Development Commission, for example, had set up a Rural Industries Bureau in 1921, which became the Council for Small Industries in Rural Areas (COSIRA) in 1947. They were the main agencies responsible for promoting the rural economy, sponsoring employers of not more than twenty skilled workers who wanted to set up or expand in a rural area where the local population did not exceed 10,000. But for many years COSIRA was a gently-flowing backwater of the Civil Service. It acquired a reputation for supporting quaint rustic crafts which, while suitably picturesque for urban sensibilities, were hardly a dynamic force in transforming rural employment opportunities.

In 1974, however, a determined attempt was made to revitalize COSIRA. Small businesses were not only becoming politically more fashionable, but their role in economic development was better understood. The Highlands and Islands Development Board had also demonstrated that a mixture of 'top-down' assistance and 'bottom-up' initiative could succeed in halting decades of economic and social decline. The development agencies have therefore seen both their budgets and their workloads

increase substantially. They have also striven to change the image of rural development, pointing out that examples of spectacular success, like Laura Ashley in mid-Wales, are less representative than the patient building up of a diverse employment base, especially in the technologically advanced industries like electronics, plastics and information technology. Recently the Development Commission has been instrumental in designating Rural Development Areas, where special assistance is offered to local businesses. They are located in remoter rural areas which suffer from continuing problems of poverty and unemployment.

Predictably this more active role has often brought the rural development agencies into conflict with village preservation societies and other environmental groups, which have been suspicious of their plans to build new workshops and warehouses in hitherto wholly agricultural areas. One effect of this has been a tendency to place advance factory units and small trading estate developments in small towns and larger villages rather than in the remoter rural hinterlands. Much can be achieved, however, by careful design and sensitive siting. A favourite solution has been to use the site of disused railway stations and goods yards, one of the best-known examples being at Bakewell in Derbyshire, where the dilapidated former railway station has been restored and brought back into use, with new workshops erected on the former forecourt and coalyard.

Developments like these offer a vivid example of just how much the economy of rural Britain is changing. Although for centuries the basis of the rural economy was agriculture, in many rural areas today this is no longer the case – and is likely to be even less so in the future. Supporting the rural economy simply by supporting agriculture will no longer do. And support for agriculture is likely, as we have seen, to decline anyway. Yet without a buoyant rural economy village communities and the countryside itself will decay and die: look at what happened to Lower Kingcombe (Chapter 5). With a further decline likely in agricultural employment, we need to encourage the growth of non-farming enterprises in the countryside.

Unfortunately planning policies in many areas have yet to catch up with these changing conditions. As we saw in Chapter 3, powerful local coalitions now exist in many rural areas to keep *any* kind of development out, including that which is necessary to maintain the vitality of the local economy. Thus the *idea*, if not the formality, of Green Belt designation has spread across vast areas of rural Britain. This is all the more tragic given that the future growth of rural Britain will not be provided by agriculture nor even by forestry, but by manufacturing and service industries,

especially those in the high technology sector which do not need to be based in towns. All too often conventional planning policy and entrenched local attitudes threaten to strangle such initiatives at birth.

—— RURAL DEVELOPMENT IN PRACTICE ——

Yet much can be done. During the 1980s a number of small-scale, prototype development projects have been established in rural areas which point the way to what can be achieved. Some of them have taken advantage of the growing government support for fostering an 'enterprise culture' in modern Britain. For example, a Development of Rural Initiative, Venture and Enterprise (DRIVE) scheme was launched in Wales in 1986 offering support for property conversion or modernization and the provision of rural community facilities. In England the Development Commission's Rural Development Programmes have sought to assist the Rural Development Areas by achieving better co-ordination between the relevant public agencies – local authorities, rural community councils, tourist boards, COSIRA, water authorities and so on. The problem of integrating policies and activities to foster rural development has long been recognized as a crucial one. Not only, as we have seen, do different public agencies pull in different directions, but for the hapless small businessman seeking to establish or expand a rural enterprise the bewildering array of organizations, each with their own priorities, rules about eligibility, conditions of support, aims and objectives, can offer a considerable disincentive.

In recent years there has therefore been a strong demand to provide 'one-stop shopping' for grant-aided rural development, whether on-farm or off-farm, inside or outside a designated area. Picture, if you can, the small businessman who is located in a Less Favoured Area, which also is an Environmentally Sensitive Area, inside a National Park, part of a Rural Development Area and surrounded by a Site of Special Scientific Interest. Can he convert a disused barn into time-sharing holiday flats? How would he know whom to ask?

Such questions have become more pertinent as farmers, for example, have been encouraged to diversify and develop non-farming sources of income on their farms. On the one hand a multitude of public agencies offer a tempting range of grants and subsidies; but on the other hand a multitude of public agencies (sometimes the same ones!) designate a range of constraints. Confused? Well, so are many rural inhabitants. Everyone agrees that better co-ordination and even integration is not only valuable

but essential. But each organization also has its own turf to defend and interests to protect. In the rural development scheme supermarket there are tempting goodies on display, which all too often the locals can see but not touch.

Two examples of what can be achieved may provide some encouragement at this point. One is organized through the public sector, the other stems from a private initiative. Both, though, depend upon a sensible, constructive and even enthusiastic marriage of public and private enterprise.

——— MONYASH, DERBYSHIRE ———

Monyash is a small village in the White Peak of Derbyshire, inside the Peak District National Park and a few miles to the east of the main Ashbourne to Buxton road. Along with its near-neighbour, Longnor, the village has, since 1981, been the site of an interesting experiment in Integrated Rural Development (IRD).

Integrated Rural Development was a favoured strategy of the World Bank during the 1960s to foster development in the rural areas of the Third World. It was subsequently abandoned. How a failed policy journeyed from south-east Asia or sub-Saharan Africa to the distinctly more bracing climate of the Derbyshire Peak District will doubtless one day be told, but a clue is that it arrived via Brussels in the form of an EEC grant. It should be emphasized that the Peak District IRD is only an experiment and is still being evaluated. Nevertheless it has attracted a great deal of attention as a possible way forward for community development across the country as a whole.

MONYASH, DERBYSHIRE: ONCE A LEAD-MINING VILLAGE, NOW REVIVING
ONCE MORE THROUGH A MIXTURE OF AGRICULTURE AND TOURISM

The idea behind IRD is that the social, economic and environmental aspects of development policy should be considered *together* rather than separately. This particularly applies where active public intervention is necessary to halt the decline of an area and to revitalize the local community. By integrating what could otherwise be separate activities it is hoped that, at least they will not be counter-productive, and more hopefully, they will allow benefits to be obtained simultaneously. In other words the community development whole will be greater than the sum of its parts. In Derbyshire a working definition of IRD was adopted involving three basic principles:

- Interdependence – a 'policy package' was custom-designed for the area which aimed to promote harmony between the different interests involved.
- Individuality – local circumstances were not only to be taken into account but were the overriding criteria for the project. It was very much a 'bottom-up' approach.
- Involvement – local communities were to be directly involved in shaping their future destinies. The keynotes were self-help and the harnessing of local skills. The appointed Project Officer was to be an 'enabler', not a leader.

Within this context the IRD project was designed to boost the vitality of the area by dovetailing the support for agriculture, conservation and local economic development. It was run out of the Peak Park Planning Board Offices in nearby Bakewell, but ten organizations administered the project via a Steering Group. A central part of the experiment was the agreement of the relevant public agencies to allow their support to be pooled via a 'Trial Alternative Grant' (TAG) scheme – the prospective kitty which formed the basis of the one-stop shopping.

Monyash was the first trial area to be set up. The village is a former centre of the local lead mining industry, but is now heavily dependent upon farming. The area has an extremely well-preserved historic landscape of small, stone-walled fields, some of which date back for 400 years. They present a most attractive landscape mosaic, breaking up what would otherwise tend to be a somewhat bleak and open prospect. One of the most important dales for wildlife conservation lies partly in the parish.

The village is attractive, but had made little effort to provide facilities for visitors, despite its proximity to a number of popular locations within the Peak. There is a strong desire in Monyash not to commercialize the village, something which is shared by both the older-established village families and by recently-arrived commuters and second-home owners. So the mainstay of the local economy has remained farming – principally small, family-run dairy farms on the margin of viability and threatened by declining returns.

IRD in Monyash centred around three types of scheme. Participation was entirely voluntary and participants were free to drop out or join in once they were under way. Community schemes related to any facility that would benefit the population of the village. Examples included a youth club, a play area, a new village hall and a car park. A farming and land management scheme enabled management grants to be paid which conserved important features of the existing landscape – limestone walls, flower-rich fields, copses of trees, etc. Unlike the Ministry of Agriculture grants they were available to all farmers, irrespective of size. Conversely grants were withheld for 'improvements' deemed detrimental to the local environment, even where they were eligible for ministry support. The third scheme involved business development and included barn conversions for campsites and small business units, new business developments and tourist-related activities.

INTEGRATED RURAL DEVELOPMENT IN MONYASH HAS
ASSISTED BOTH THE MAN-MADE AND THE NATURAL ENVIRONMENT

Early indications of the results have been encouraging. During the first three years ten new full-time jobs were created together with several more part-time jobs. Many existing businesses were helped to improve their income. The average cost per job created was less than £3000 – an extraordinarily low figure compared with urban development examples – and an important side-effect was that a number of derelict and run-down buildings in the villages were restored and improved. Moreover, twenty-five different community projects were assisted, including an award-winning village hall in Monyash. More facilities induced more community activity. Old traditions, like well dressing, were revived – and brought an income from tourists. The farming and land management scheme has demonstrated that conservation can be incorporated into farming practices, given the right incentives. Lessons learned in Monyash were later used in the establishment of the nationwide system of ESAs.

In Monyash IRD has proved cheap and effective. The drawbacks have been relatively few. Some of the local people grumble about the project having attracted in newcomers, but this, as we have seen elsewhere, would probably have happened anyway. There have been one or two individual cases of what might be called 'grantsmanship' where public support has turned into private benefit, but these are a small minority. Some of the 'traditions' have been somewhat forced and 'community' somewhat self-consciously celebrated, but these have been a relatively small price to pay for a discernible resuscitation.

The more difficult question to assess is not so much whether IRD has worked in Monyash, but whether it can be applied across the countryside as a whole. Third World experience is relevant here. It was a pronounced feature of IRD in the developing countries that it relied heavily on the personal qualities, commitment and expertise of the IRD project officer, who, however self-effacing, was the impressario of the various schemes. When he or she moved on or moved out IRD proved difficult to sustain. Even in Monyash it is widely acknowledged that the initial success has been due to the individuals, even a single individual, who acted as catalyst. This is a rather fragile basis on which to build community development. Sustainability was the undoing of Third World IRD. The same problem could afflict the Peak District.

IRD essentially involves a series of valuable and worthwhile minor works schemes. Taken on their own terms they can produce tangible benefits to the local community. Whether they add up to a rural development strategy is another matter. IRD is enormously vulnerable to changes over which the local community has no control. More and more aspects of our daily lives are decided upon by individuals and

organizations far away from where we live and work. Global economic crisis, multi-national organizations, rising oil prices, the international debt crisis undermined IRD in the Third World; in Monyash dairy quotas, ratecapping, government expenditure cuts – each could blow IRD away on the winds that sweep across the Peak. IRD is certainly valuable at the local level. It also exposes some of the absurdities of what passes for rural policy in Britain. But it is no substitute for a properly integrated rural development strategy.

——— ARDINGTON, OXFORDSHIRE ———

Ardington lies just east of Wantage in Oxfordshire on the edge of the vale of the White Horse and close to the foot of the North Downs. It is an estate village, part of the Lockinge Estate, one of the last Victorian estates put together in the latter half of the nineteenth century. In the past the estate contained as many as 850 inhabitants and even after the Second World War there were 700, but now it is down to 500. The estate itself once employed 350 people, but this has now been reduced to just fifty. In this respect the Lockinge Estate has followed the trend of labour-shedding which is apparent in agriculture up and down the country.

Ardington could therefore have become a ghost village, but in the early 1970s the estate decided that something must be done to provide alternative employment in the village and to revitalize the life of the community. The estate has a long history of innovation and attending to the social needs of its two villages, Ardington and Lockinge. It consulted the local people, via the parish councils, about what they would like to see done and they came up with three objectives. First, they wanted to see the village amenities – schools, shops, church, pub, etc. – retained and improved. Second, they wanted to see the population increased (to around 700) which they felt was the minimum necessary to sustain the vitality of the villages. And lastly they wanted the people who would come into the village to have something in common with those already there. In other words they wanted newcomers who, like them, worked in the village.

Ardington was, and still is, a working village. Since most of its inhabitants were associated with the estate, home and work intermingled. A farmyard was located in the middle of the village and villagers were quite accustomed to all the comings and goings associated with daily farming operations. So when the estate began to consider attracting alternative sources of employment into Ardington, not only did the conversion of redundant farm buildings suggest itself but, for the local people, this did not represent a very great transition. There was no necessity to convince a sceptical

A FULL RANGE OF LOCAL SERVICES ARE IMPORTANT
TO MAINTAIN VITALITY OF THE VILLAGE:
THE GENERAL STORES AT ARDINGTON, OXFORDSHIRE

group of newcomers who had come to Ardington for a quiet, settled retirement. The estate was merely providing a different kind of employment to the agricultural jobs which had traditionally predominated, but supplying them in light industries and services which offered the prospect of growth rather than decline.

The estate administration managed to convince the local planning authority that its plans were both necessary and viable. On the former Home Farm it created one very small workshop. Today a former Victorian stables and associated farm buildings house sixteen small business units – and more are planned. The businesses themselves are very diverse, ranging from injection-moulded plastics and computing systems to a clock-maker, a furniture restorer and a stonemason. Together they form a rural trading estate cum craft centre housed in attractive buildings on a pleasant site. Rents are not cheap, but the scheme is a commercial and social success. It is also unobtrusively designed and makes good use of premises which might otherwise be under-used and semi-derelict.

New people coming to work in Ardington needed to be housed, so in 1974 the family which owns the Lockinge Estate established a charitable housing association in order to house elderly people and to provide starter homes for the young. In this way it was hoped to maintain a social balance in the village. Those who retired would not have to move away; local housing was available for the sons and daughters of village families; and those working on the trading estate would not have to live outside with possibly divisive consequences.

Having dealt with employment and housing, the maintenance of a full range of amenities and services then followed. The two estate villages now contain three shops, two churches, a pub, one school with education up to the age of 11, a sports club and two village halls. They are thriving, working communities. Integrated rural development has been achieved in Ardington without any conscious attempt to introduce it via a publicly-supported scheme.

The full potential of the planned development for Ardington has yet to be achieved. The estate is only half way through using its stock of redundant farm buildings, and reckons that current employment levels could be doubled. It has also recognized that 'ordinary industrial users' offer a greater spread of employment and training possibilities than the more quaintly rustic craft artisans. More recently there are proposals to undertake conversions for office use which will offer high rates of employment – and rents – per square foot.

Why has community development in Ardington been so successful? Clearly being adjacent to the M4 corridor helps: this has been one of the fastest-growing parts of

HOME FARM, ARDINGTON: THE FORMER STABLES HAVE BEEN CONVERTED TO A RANGE OF SMALL
BUSINESS UNITS. THEY INCLUDE BOTH TRADITIONAL CRAFTS LIKE WATCH REPAIR,
STONEMASONRY AND FURNITURE RESTORATION, TOGETHER WITH HI-TECH DEVELOPMENTS
SUCH AS COMPUTING EQUIPMENT AND INJECTION-MOULDED PLASTICS

PROVIDING A DIVERSITY OF HOUSING ENABLES A SOCIAL BALANCE TO BE ACHIEVED IN
THE VILLAGE COMMUNITY. ALL TOO OFTEN, HOWEVER, MARKET PRESSURES DICTATE HIGH-COST,
LOW-DENSITY DEVELOPMENTS SUCH AS THIS IN ARDINGTON. THE VARIED TEXTURE
OF THE ENGLISH LANDSCAPE: HOW MUCH ARE WE PREPARED TO PAY TO MAINTAIN IT?

Britain during the 1980s. But the key factor has been the capacity to produce an integrated development strategy which encompasses social, commercial and, indeed, environmental objectives. This has come about by virtue of the patronage of the estate: clearly an economic development and land use strategy is that much easier to implement when the control of an area is vested in one institution. There is not the fragmentation of landowners, homeowners, etc. that there is in Monyash. But there is surely a lesson to be learned here. The integration of agriculture, conservation and economic development can be shown to work in practice. The evidence is there to be seen. If we look back to Chapter 3 for a moment, Ardington could have become a Shilton – gentrified and exclusive; or it could have become Allenheads – dilapidated and in danger of total decay. Instead, through far-sighted and imaginative planning, it remains a thriving, working community. It seems a worthy successor to the Victorian tradition of enlightened self-interest in estate management.

PUTTING THE PIECES TOGETHER

In their different ways Monyash and Ardington show how the diverse strands of rural change can be brought together in closer harmony. In addition they both demonstrate how, in today's countryside, the rural economy cannot be left solely in the hands of agriculture. Fortunately there are some signs that traditional barriers are breaking down.

In March 1987, the Ministry of Agriculture launched a Farming and Rural Enterprise package to encourage farmers to diversify away from their traditional farming activity and to exploit the assets of their holdings to supplement their income. Spurred on by the threats of cutbacks in farm production, there might be many farms and estates which might like to follow the Ardington example. This in turn would mean viewing the farm as a multi-purpose enterprise. Agriculture, conservation, diversified economic activity – all would form part of a development strategy for the farm and, by implication, the rural community as a whole.

With the assistance of a specially-created Countryside Policy Review Panel, the Countryside Commission has recently outlined the ways in which an integrated approach to the future of rural Britain might proceed. As the panel's report concluded:

> The natural beauty of the countryside and the health of rural communities are interdependent. The attractiveness of the countryside depends on the care with which it is managed by farmers, foresters and all who own buildings. If the livelihood of rural people is undermined, the countryside itself will become less attractive. Caring for the countryside is likely to become an increasing source of rural income and employment. At the same time, many rural communities benefit from income generated by visitors and tourists who come to enjoy the countryside. So it is in the national interest, and not simply in the rural interest, that there should continue to be a thriving countryside.

THE COUNTRYSIDE IN QUESTION

The panel exhorts local authorities and central government to prepare Rural Development Strategies which would encompass economic and social development, agricultural, environmental and recreational objectives. It also suggests that the system of farm advice should be overhauled and broadened to take account of such objectives and that individual farm plans should no longer be concerned solely with agricultural requirements, but should reflect these multi-purpose aims.

Somehow we have so organized matters that these different strands of rural life have developed not merely separately, but as though they were in conflict with each other. It does not have to be like that. In the landscape the patchwork of fields may look like a mosaic, but they come together to offer a satisfactory whole. Similarly, when it comes to considering the fragmented way we organize rural policy, it is necessary, for the countryside to function properly, to put the pieces together. What we need is not a rigid blueprint to be slapped down on each and every rural community, but an assessment of priorities and guidance for the future.

WITHOUT A THRIVING SOCIAL AND ECONOMIC FABRIC LANDSCAPES
LIKE THIS WILL DISAPPEAR: THE YORKSHIRE DALES

Some things can be predicted. In the countryside of the future, agriculture's role will have been reduced. The number of farmers who earn their living exclusively from the production of food will be much smaller. So will the number of farmers whom we are prepared to encourage to grow more food. Some we will fund to maintain the populations of the remoter rural areas; others will be paid to maintain the rural landscape through 'staged' farming with farmers acting as resident sceneshifters for visitors and tourists; still others will manage the land to bring the visitors in for leisure and recreation – or to keep them out in favour of the preservation of wildlife habitats and the protection of rare species. But it is inevitable that the role of agriculture in the countryside will change quite substantially.

So we return to the questions with which we began. What kind of countryside do we want? And how can we develop the right kind of policies which will guide the British countryside into the twenty-first century? Forty years of assumptions which have influenced public policy are now coming to an end, but so far we have had little debate over what is to replace them. What *is* the balance we wish to see between agriculture, forestry, conservation, recreation and rural economic development? What we conspicuously lack at the moment is a strategy to guide policy-makers, planners and the rural inhabitants themselves over the balance to be struck between these competing claims.

For the last decade the concern for conservation has so dominated our thinking about the countryside that these more fundamental issues have crept up on us almost by surprise. Conservation alone cannot provide the social and economic vitality on which a thriving countryside depends. Rural Britain must be allowed to develop and grow if it is to survive. Now that productive agriculture no longer needs so much land the opportunity is there to develop an innovative approach to rural development. This will require a strengthening of strategic planning for the future so that broad guidelines can be set down to assist local decision-making within the rural community. This may well involve a progressive shift *away* from supporting food production and *towards* promoting appropriate development, housing, public services and a better social balance within the rural village.

This would be a small price to pay for the retention of a beautiful countryside and the revitalization of the rural community. But if the opportunity is not to be lost, a national debate on the future of our countryside has to be undertaken soon. The countryside is much too important for its future to be decided by default.

FURTHER READING

The following list offers only a few of the very many books now available for those wishing to pursue an interest in rural change. The Open University offers a post-experience course on 'The Changing Countryside' and its two accompanying books, *The Changing Countryside*, edited by John Blunden and Nigel Curry (Croom Helm, 1985) and *Critical Countryside*, edited by John Blunden and Graham Turner (BBC Publications, 1985), provide a valuable introduction. Two of my earlier books, *Green and Pleasant Land?* (Wildwood House, second edition, 1986) and *Country Life* (Weidenfeld, 1987) cover similar ground in more detail than has been possible here.

There are few up-to-date and easily available accounts of British farming, but one which has contributed considerably to recent debates on the direction of farming policy is John Bowers and Paul Cheshire, *Agriculture, the Countryside and Land Use* (Methuen, 1983).

Environmental issues have dominated recent discussions of the countryside. A comprehensive list of books would be a very long one indeed, but notable classics include Nan Fairbrother, *New Lives, New Landscapes* (Pelican, 1977), Marion Shoard, *The Theft of the Countryside* (Temple Smith, 1981), Richard Mabey, *The Common Ground* (Hutchinson, 1980) and Oliver Rackham, *The History of the Countryside* (Dent, 1986). Recent contributions to the policy arguments include Charlie Pye-Smith and Richard North, *Working the Land* (Temple Smith, 1984), Philip Lowe *et al.*, *Countryside Conflicts* (Temple Smith/Gower, 1986), and Ann and Malcolm MacEwan, *Greenprints for the Countryside?* (Allen and Unwin, 1987). Marion Shoard has recently returned to the attack with *This Land is Our Land* (Paladin, 1987).

One of the frustrations for the general reader is that much of the discussion of the issues raised in this book tends to take place in reports, conference papers and other such 'fugitive' literature. One recent publication which brings much of this discussion together is *New Opportunities for the Countryside*, the report of the Countryside Policy Review Panel (Countryside Commission, 1987).